Furry
Spirits

Furry Spirits

The Beautiful Souls of our Animal Friends

GLYNIS AMY ALLEN

ISBN 978-1-910027-48-6

Typesetting by Wordzworth Ltd
www.wordzworth.com

Cover design by Titanium Design Ltd
www.titaniumdesign.co.uk

Cover image:
Bonzai by kind permission of Sylvie Gotti

Images by the author and courtesy of
www.creativecommons.org

Published by Local Legend
www.local-legend.co.uk

Acknowledgements

I am very grateful to my husband Frank, my children Karen and Neil and their partners Rehaz and Kate Amelia, and to my friend Sharon, for their support and guidance.

Thank you, all the wonderful people who have contributed stories for this book, and my publisher Nigel Peace for his guidance and patience.

For permission to quote from their work, the publisher thanks sincerely:

Tony Ortzen, Editor of *Psychic News* magazine (*www.psychicnews.org.uk*), and

Janine Wilbraham, author of *Can You Hear Me?* (Local Legend Publishing).

Disclaimer

The personal names of some of the people and animals referred to in this book have been changed to preserve their privacy.

Other Books By This Author

Ghosts of the NHS (978-1-910027-34-90
The Angels Beside Us (978-1-910027-39-4)
both available in paperback and as eBooks

www.local-legend.co.uk

About The Author

"I have been blessed," says Glynis, "with amazing spiritual gifts, especially clairvoyance, passed down to me by my Grandma Mac. She spoke with spirits and angels and taught me that I could always reach out to them. It has been natural, and a privilege, for me to carry on her work."

During a career of over three decades in the NHS, much of this as a senior nurse in A&E wards, Glynis had almost daily encounters with spirit doctors and spirit families gathering to guide their deceased loved ones onwards. She told these stories in her debut, bestselling book *Ghosts of the NHS*.

When her nursing career was cut short by an injury, it soon became clear that Spirit had other plans for Glynis and she has devoted herself to working as a clairvoyant medium, in constant contact with the souls of the afterlife, both human and animal.

Indeed, Glynis is a passionate supporter of animal charities and has developed a special personal link with our furry friends. In this book, she not only tells many fascinating and evidential stories of animal survival after death – giving compassionate guidance on how to deal with the grief of their loss – but also describes the amazing healing and psychic abilities of animals.

Be reassured that your pet's spirit certainly lives on after their passing, and that you can reach out and connect with them again.

Her website is
www.glynisallenpsychic.com

Contents

Introduction

We are a nation of animal lovers and we would do anything for our 'furry babies' who give us such happiness and companionship. Animals come in all shapes, sizes and types and when we lose them it can be devastating. So this book is about both the spirit lives of animals and their wonderful abilities, informed by my experiences as a clairvoyant medium and by the joy of having pets myself and the sadness of their loss.

In my psychic work I have located many lost or stolen animals and communicated with many who have passed over the Rainbow Bridge. I can see deceased pets and bring their owners a message. If you have lost a much-loved pet, I hope these stories will give you reassurance that they are safe and well, being loved and cared for by celestial healers. As you grieve, please accept my deepest sympathy.

All lives come to an end but perhaps reading about the transition from this Earth life to the next world will bring you some emotional healing. I have included a section on how to cope with loss, based on the Kübler-Ross model that has helped me personally over the years. There is also an explanation of how other pets cope with the loss of their mate.

You may even already be aware that some pets do come back to their earthly homes to see their owners, leaving a scent or even the clatter of their food bowl. I have described a few signs to watch out for. And I have some intriguing stories to tell about quite bizarre behaviour, about spirit animal guides and their work, and about the special psychic abilities of some animals helping us in this life.

I hope you enjoy reading this book and that it brings you some pleasure and the reassurance you may need.

1

Roland Rat's Legacy

Some people don't have the usual sort of pets. Roland the white rat had lived on a local caravan park with three other rats. His owner was what one might call 'quirky', with piercings in her nose, ears and fingers, multi-coloured hair that looked like rats' tails, and a big tattoo of a rat that covered her arm. But I am never shocked by people's appearance and preferences because I love meeting people, especially quirky ones like Vanda.

She told me that her Grandad Herbert had been the local rat catcher on a big estate in the south and when she went there during the holidays she would help him with his work. The place was in disorder, mouldy and with holes in the walls and overrun with vermin. Grandad only had a forked stick and a bag to catch the rats. He would then put them in a cage and release them five miles away. But she laughed and said, "They always found their way back, so Grandad was never out of a job."

One day he was summoned by his employer, a nasty man, because someone had seen him releasing the rats so Herbert was sacked. It was Christmas Day, though, and he was allowed to have his Christmas dinner with all the other servants. They were all sitting down, singing and making merry, when Cook let out a scream because two rats were on the table; Herbert grabbed one but it bit him and he contracted Weil's disease (a form of leptospirosis) and died. What an irony. When his home was being cleared, Vanda found twenty white albino rats in different cages; they'd had to have them put to sleep but she kept three of them, Roland, Athena and Monty, and took them home.

"You think I am weird, don't you, with my purple hair and piercings and love of rats?" she said accusingly.

"Not at all," I assured her. "My own sister had a white rat that she adored – and no, I don't judge people on their appearance. But why have you come for a reading?"

"Someone has poisoned Roland and I want to know who it was." Then she started to cry and said, "I used to sing him and the others to sleep at night. They're my babies. But I loved Roland the best."

With that, she brought out a large jewellery box… I thought, 'Please let there not be a rat in there', but there was. Roland was laid out on the red silk lining, wearing a small dickie bow and covered with a black silk handkerchief. I thought to myself, 'Any minute now I am going to wake up from this dream.'

I felt this reading could be difficult because it was clear that Vanda wanted to blame the caravan site owner. "He said that if he saw my rats loose, he would kill them."

I began by using my Witch Tarot cards because I find them good for interpretation and easy to work with. The first card out was The Devil, so a mischief-maker was around who was jealous of Vanda's love for her rats. "I know who that is," she said, "I was right." But I told her not to jump to conclusions as this person might be innocent; we should see what the rest of the reading brought. In a vision, I was then shown a man with as many piercings as Vanda had, a dubious looking man, alongside the card of betrayal, the Nine of Swords.

"You're accusing the wrong person," I said, but she was having none of it at the moment. Tellingly, the next card was The Lovers

– not always a lovely one as it can also point to betrayal and the jealousy of three in a relationship. I saw the man with piercings again, picking up a white rat. I am always honest with my clients and had to tell Vanda that someone was cheating on their partner. Her response did shock me, though.

"That's me," she said. "I cheated on my boyfriend with his best friend, but we're still living together in the caravan." She took out a photo of the man and I knew that it was him who had poisoned Roland. She shook her head and said, "He would never do that, he loves them."

However, the reading continued with The Moon, the card of deceit. I had to tell Vanda, "Well, you have cheated on your boyfriend but he has also cheated on you." She agreed that she had suspected it, that she had found someone's underwear, but hadn't said anything because she didn't want to lose him. "You would stay with him even knowing that he poisoned Roland?" I asked.

"Yes, but I'm going to make him pay for what he's done."

If you'll forgive the phrase, there was a real twist in the tail of this story. The last card out was The Empress, which predicts new projects as well as fertility, and in my mind I was shown another white rat with a belly full of babies. I told her that one of her rats was pregnant but she shook her head, saying that she didn't have any females. "You'd better check when you get home," I smiled.

Vanda 'phoned me later that night and said, "When I got home there was a big bunch of flowers waiting for me and a baby white rat. My boyfriend wrote a note saying he was so sorry he'd killed Roland. He'd been out of his mind with jealousy and wanted me to forgive him."

Fate certainly works in mysterious ways. This couple later got married and started to breed albino rats, which apparently are very popular!

A couple came to see me asking whether their dogs Pinkie and Perky had gone to Heaven and were still together. The lady began by telling me that they were French bulldogs costing thousands of pounds, but more importantly, "They were my girls, my babies."

As she started to cry, I was explaining to them that Archangel Fhelyai and St Francis, the patron saint of animals, would be looking after their two furry friends when two beautiful little dogs appeared at her feet, wagging their tails.

As we waited for the lady to calm down, her husband told me the tale. They had taken the dogs to the seaside because they loved running into the water, but Pinkie had started to drift out to sea with Perky following her sister. "My wife was screaming for help but there was no-one about because it was a cold, windy day and the sea was choppy." He started to cry too. "They just drifted out of sight. We have come here today hoping you could find out if they died, and where they are now."

The dogs were around my ankles now so that was definite, yes, they had died and were now furry spirits. Both dogs were looking up at me and telepathically passing on the message that they had drowned and had been picked up together by a fisherman, who was still looking after their bodies in his shed while he tried to find the owners.

I told the couple this and also described the dogs' pink collars decorated with little pigs; I was also shown their food bowls, one with 'Pinkie' inscribed and the other 'Perky' but with the name spelled wrongly. The lady gasped, "Unbelievable!" and put her hand over her mouth. Then an unmistakable smell drifted up around us all and she said, "That's our Pinkie all right, she was always farting like that." It was a struggle for me not to laugh.

I was also able to tell them where the fisherman lived and a couple of weeks later the lady 'phoned me to say, "You were right. We've brought them back home and have decided to get them stuffed." This might seem bizarre, but they were their special 'babies' so who are we to judge?

It's easy to understand that many people become very attached to their pets, but sometimes the relationship can be taken perhaps a little too far... A young couple came to see me and the lady said, "We have lost our baby girl and we want to know if she's okay." I felt I should use my Angel cards in this case since Spirit usually then comes forward straightaway, but I had mixed feelings about this couple who didn't seem as terribly upset about the loss of a child as I'd expect.

I asked the child's name and the lady said, "Sheba." Hmm, I suppose there are plenty of unusual names nowadays. What happened next took my breath away as the most beautiful golden Labrador appeared beside me. I was confused now but kept quiet and carried on until the man asked, "Who looks after animals in Heaven?" Ah, their 'baby girl' was this much-loved dog.

I told them about the Rainbow Bridge and how animals are assessed and then looked after in different places according to how they'd been treated on Earth. When I told them about the golden Labrador at our feet the lady put her hands to her mouth and said, "That's our baby girl, Sheba."

We began the reading with the Archangel Azrael card: 'Your loved ones in Heaven are doing fine. Let go of worries and feel their love around you.' I also had a message that Sheba was passing on to me for her 'Mummy and Daddy'.

'You both seem to have lost yourselves in grief,' she said. 'Your mood is dim, your auras are dark.'

"What do dogs know about auras?" The lady seemed a bit sceptical now.

"Your girl is being helped on the Other Side. In fact, she is with your brother, Colin."

"No," she said, "my brother isn't there, he was frightened of dogs." So Colin now chipped in himself.

'I saw our Mum crying when she went shopping and told that woman she was buying those things for our Colin.'

The lady across the table just stared at me and said that this was exactly what had happened two weeks ago. But she still wasn't convinced – did she think I was in the queue in that shop behind her Mum? – and insisted I should describe her brother. Taking a couple of discreet deep breaths, I asked my guide Black Feather for a bit of extra help. I was shown a youth of about fourteen years-old in a wheelchair as he had spina bifida; he was clutching an Action Man figure. I was then given the date he passed over and relayed all this information to them.

The second card was Angel Yvonne: 'You have a special bond with animals. Your pets on Earth and in Heaven are watched over by the angels and all the animals you have loved continue to be with you, like guardian angels.' Sheba then showed me the lower half of her body where there was a large swelling on her left leg and the couple confirmed that, yes, it had been a tumour that spread.

"What are Guardian Angels?"

"How did you know Colin's name?"

"How do you communicate with animals?"

This was turning into an interrogation, so I just told them that I connect with animals the same as I connect with humans and that I have a wolf and an owl as my animal spirit guides. The looked at me as though I was crackers, then thankfully said, "There is so much to understand. We will have to come again, this is amazing." Sheba then stepped in again with more evidence, showing me a scene of this couple both kissing her head as her soul left her body; she said it brought her great comfort that they had made the decision not to keep her in pain but let her go.

The next card brought the message, 'Have faith and hope, there is something new on the horizon that you cannot see yet.' I thought about this for a moment and then Sheba herself showed me a vision of this couple looking at chocolate-coloured puppies. The man confirmed that she'd had four such puppies a few months before, and I continued, "One of those puppies is coming back to you." The lady was still finding it hard to take all this in and shook her head.

"No way, we vetted all the people who took the pups. And not only that, we've kept in touch with them and all the dogs are happy."

Undeterred, I carried on with the reading and drew the Archangel Raphael card. This archangel is the healer in the angelic hierarchy so I said, "I feel this card has come out because you both need healing since Sheba passed over." Sheba herself showed me a lump behind her ear and the man confirmed it; they had only noticed it when she was put to sleep.

Colin wanted to get back into the conversation now. 'I wasn't scared of Sheba,' he objected. 'I taught her to fetch her ball. She was so gentle as she picked it up and chucked it onto my lap.'

"No, that's not right," I was told, "we never saw that."

I was getting a bit fed up with their negativity and the reading had already taken twice as long as the normal one hour, so I just said, "I would check with your Mum, then, because she looked after Colin and Sheba while you both worked. And please check out the puppies' owners."

The following day the man rang to say, "Guess what—" of course, I knew what was coming "—you were right. Dad did teach Sheba to fetch her ball to Colin. And an email was waiting for us saying that the owners of one of the puppies are emigrating so would we like their pup back..." He went on to say that they'd been fascinated by the reading and apologised for going over the time.

I was just glad it had been successful, although that night I was exhausted! Sometimes, however, my readings bring a little light relief.

A young woman told me that her cats had been missing for four days and she thought they had been taken from her garden. She had informed the police and the RSPCA and put posters up around the area asking for information. I started the reading using Tarot cards and the first one out was The Hanged Man, which means 'confusion'. It is commonplace here that the client has placed themselves in a difficult position, yet The Hanged Man indicates peace and calm, all will be well.

"Have both cats been neutered?" I asked, not sure why that came into my head. She looked at me horrified and said, "I would never do that to my boys." I had to stifle a laugh when the next card came out: The Lovers!

I asked Black Feather to come forward with some information about these cats and was given a vision – accompanied by the most horrendous howling – of the cats sitting on a wall alongside other cats, all looking towards a bungalow. There in the window was the most beautiful Burmese golden honey female cat. The cats outside then started to fight and the fur was flying.

"No-one has stolen your cats," I told the lady. "They are two miles away, sitting on a wall and howling."

"Are you being funny?" she replied, offended. "It's no laughing matter. My cats are lost."

I told her that they had caught the scent of a female cat who was in season and were fighting over her with other local toms. Cautiously, she accepted that this might be true and asked me where they were, taking out her car keys. This was my last reading of the day so I offered to go with her; it wasn't far and I knew the house because I sometimes walk my dogs nearby and had seen this princess cat myself. As we approached the house we saw four cats sitting on the wall looking like a picture postcard; there was one black, two ginger and a tortoiseshell.

"The little sods," my client said, "look at them, fur on their heads missing and blood around their mouths. I thought you were having me on and I'm so sorry for doubting you." Well, nothing surprises me anymore and I trust my spirit guide one hundred per cent when he shows me something.

She picked up one of her cats but he bit her and was struggling in her arms, so she got him by the scruff of the neck and chucked him into the car while the other one ran off. It was like an episode of *You've Been Framed* with the cat in the car howling at the top of his voice all the while. Eventually the other one came back and I sneaked up behind him, grabbed him and put him in the car.

The lady called me a couple of days later to say, "They won't be roaming anymore, they've been neutered." But about six months later she rang, laughing this time, because they had gone missing again and she found them in exactly the same place, just sitting quietly on the wall hoping to catch a glance of the princess.

"I keep them indoors now," she said. "If they go out they'll be on the washing line. And I'm going to get two female cats so my boys won't want to roam."

I've often wondered whether she now has howling cats outside on her own wall, but I guess as long as she and her furry family are happy that's all that matters. The best bit of this story is that her boys were named Joe and… Randy.

Sometimes the sadness at the loss of a pet can haunt us for years – and even reveal dark secrets. One lady was still deeply upset by what had happened to her pet rabbit thirty years before, when she was just a child of twelve years-old. The rabbit was a big white fluffy one called Angel. She had gone to school one day and when she came home the rabbit was gone. When she asked her parents about Angel, sure that someone must have taken her, they both denied any knowledge of the missing pet.

Sometimes I get a gut feeling in my stomach when something bad is happening and I felt that now as I started the reading. You will know by now that I usually begin by using the Tarot and then Spirit will jump in.

The Nine of Swords is often associated with despair and anxiety about a situation, which tallied with this situation, but at first nothing else was coming through to me. Where was Black Feather? Next we had The Devil card which appears when a situation is dragging you down and you feel helpless to change it. Moreover, it may carry an aspect of secrecy – plans being made behind one's back – and depicts a mischief-maker who is only thinking of themselves.

I now picked up my Faden quartz crystal for clarity and what I was shown was beyond belief. How could I tell this woman what Spirit were showing me? Yet I always have to be truthful.

"The vision I have been shown is not nice, I'm afraid. Do you want me to continue?" She nodded, saying that she had an inkling of what might be coming.

At that moment, I heard crying and a spirit lady stood behind my client. She said, 'Tell her it was him, not me. I fought with him but he took her.' Then, confusingly, a spirit man came forward actually holding Angel in his arms. Should I really tell her the truth? Black Feather said, 'That is why she has come, for confirmation.'

"It's awful," I said to the lady, "what I could tell you. Do you want me to go on?"

"I bloody well knew it," she replied, ahead of me. "Yes, I am ready to hear what my parents have to say."

As I started to tell her what had happened to Angel, I felt a tickling on my legs and looked down to see Angel playing happily there. "You were very poor," I began, "and your father was out of work. You had no food. With your three brothers and two sisters, Mam and Dad were desperate and thought they had no choice. They took Angel to the butchers and came back with food for a week."

My poor client started to cry, but then we both heard a rustling and she looked down at her feet. "Good heavens," she said, "I have just seen my Angel!" It was only for a few seconds but she was so happy that her beloved pet had come back to see her. As she got up to leave, she said, "I understand now why they had to do it. Times were bad, back then. A few years later, Dad did buy me a couple more rabbits though I never felt the same about them as I did my Angel. At least I know the truth now. Thank you, it must have been hard for you to tell me." That was an understatement.

Usually, the loss of a pet is not so sinister yet it can still be due to human carelessness. I was asked to do an event involving about ten people and one of the ladies had brought her two dogs along, a Jack Russell and a pug. When it was her turn to ask a question, she said, "I have lost my dog."

At first I wasn't sure if she meant lost or passed over, but then I felt something licking my leg and looked down to see a little brown and white spirit dog looking up at me. The strange thing was that he had one brown eye and one blue. As I was telling the lady this, I heard the word 'poisoned' and the dog was foaming at the mouth, trying to tell me what had happened, and showing me coloured foil paper. This was a mystery and I couldn't work out what the little one was trying to say. Here was a much-loved dog, yet he had been poisoned?

I needed to move on with other people's readings but the little dog followed me around the room before going to sit beside her owner. When the event finished I was shattered, but still intrigued about this dog and the coloured foil. The lady approached me.

"Thank you for bringing him through. That's what I came for, and to beg his forgiveness." She told me that the family had gone out for a meal at Eastertime and there had been Easter eggs filled with chocolates left on a table. When they got back, the dog was foaming at the mouth, fitting, having eaten a whole egg with the chocolates inside. There was coloured wrapping foil all over the floor. They had rushed her to the vet who purged her, but it was too late; the chocolate had poisoned her system.

I told her that her pet was here with us now, saying to me that it was her own fault, not theirs. She had been greedy. The lady said, "If only she would send me a sign, to say that she's forgiven me." She rang me three days later to say that she had found a beautiful white feather left on her doorstep. "I can sleep peacefully now," she said, "knowing I am forgiven."

Well, no-one is perfect and we all make mistakes. The dog's owner was not to know she would climb onto the table to get to the Easter egg. But please be aware that chocolate is poisonous to dogs because it contains a chemical called theobromine that affects their central nervous system, as well as their cardiovascular and respiratory systems. The darker the chocolate, the more dangerous it is. There are substitute treats for dogs but please check the label when you buy them.

One of the terrible things of the last few years is the huge increase in thefts of pets, especially dogs. This is as devastating as it is cruel. Sometimes, though, even the most awful situations can have a happy ending.

One year, I took our Jake the fox terrier to Cruft's since his grandfather had been a champion; the management had asked me to bring him, to show people what a fox terrier puppy looked like. I got talking to a lady who was showing her spaniel. She told me she had attended one of my psychic events the year before, and rather embarrassed me with her praise. Then she told me that the dog she was showing this year was not the one she had intended to bring because Sally, who was a champion and worth a lot of money, had gone missing from her garden. She asked me if she could come for a reading, to shed light on who had taken her. She showed me a photo of Sally, who was beautifully marked.

It is always a great honour to be asked to help find a pet, but it brings a lot of responsibility and, sometimes, heartache. I used my Witch Tarot cards for this, my favourite because they seem to make the connection easier with nature and animals, and I did my usual thing of asking the four archangels to protect me and my client and for Black Feather to come forward. I was shown a vision of a man in a white coat, but this was not enough for me to say anything yet.

The Three of Swords suggests time of heartrending devastation caused by loss and betrayal. There was no nice way to put this, it was going to be a tough and emotional reading. But the good thing was that I couldn't see or feel Sally, which told me she was still alive.

The Nine of Cups was a good card next, telling me that this lady would be attending a social event within a select community. It is also known as 'the wish card' so I told the lady what to do with it and to follow the instructions very carefully. I was beginning to feel hopeful now until… The Devil appeared. As we've seen before, this is the mischief-maker.

"Someone in your circle of friends or family has taken Sally," I said. "They are not a true friend and you have been targeted."

Now my psychic work began in earnest, asking Spirit for guidance. I trust Black Feather totally as he always gives good advice, whether it be a word or a vision. But he does not always come instantly; it's as though he is testing me and saying, 'Yes, I'll come in when you really need me.' At this moment I was shown a vision of Sally in a dark blue van and another spaniel with her in a cage. I reassured my client that Sally was safe, but where was she?

Next, I saw a ferry ship and on board were other dogs, other breeds, all in cages. The people who had stolen Sally were foreign-looking, and I was shown a shamrock which suggested Ireland.

"The dogs are well looked after," I said, "and Sally is with others of the same breed. I get the names Michael and Patrick, both men are wearing white coats." The lady turned pale.

"That's my nephew and his partner. They are vets."

The Six of Wands was a fantastic card to come up now, meaning victory and an inner strength that would be needed when confronting the situation. But all obstacles encountered would be overcome. Then I was shown the man in the white coat again, removing something from Sally's neck – her identity chip. The vision developing next was tense: the ferry was not sailing, it was still docked, so I told the lady she needed to contact the police before the ferry could leave the country. "Please bear in mind," I warned her, "that this is the strength card so brute force may be necessary."

"I am just going to make some calls," she said calmly, getting up to leave the room, "and then we can carry on with the reading."

I felt it was time to change the method of clairvoyance, to use my crystals, and Archangel Chamuel is the one to call on for lost pets. I asked Chamuel to help me find Sally and to know where she was going. I was shown rays of yellow and green, and saw gold coins falling in front of my face. Then I saw the man in the white coat again only this time I could read the name of the vet's practice on his pocket! I heard the name 'County Mayo' and then part of the song from Watership Down. What on Earth?!

When the lady came back in the room I gave her all this additional information and what she said next shocked me.

"It's my nephew who owns the practice. He's the one who examines the dogs before they are shown. He has two houses, one in the UK and a farm in County Mayo where he breeds highly-prized rabbits. His father is my brother." We now had a strong lead to Sally's whereabouts.

She took a 'phone call. "They've missed the ferry and the Garda is waiting for them on the other side. Thank you for your help."

Two weeks later she told me that the Garda had followed the dark blue van to a remote farm where there where cages full of champion dogs. Her nephew and his partner had been arrested for stealing animals; Sally was in a bit of a state but she was safely back home now.

Oh, and she was pregnant! Later she gave birth to four little pups.

2

Bertha's Secrets

It's not only dogs that are stolen. And not all pets are so furry. An elderly couple came to see me having travelled a long way so I asked how they had found me.

"We read in the Mercury newspaper about how you found lost animals," the gentleman said. (I was the 'psychic columnist' for the Mercury for a few years.) "We have lost our little girl," he went on. "Bertha is a Pot-bellied pig. She has just had piglets and she was stolen the day before yesterday." The Vietnamese Pot-bellied is a traditional breed of small, domesticated pig, black with short legs and a low-hanging belly, hence the name. Bertha was not only this couple's 'baby' but also a champion, so she and her piglets were worth a lot of money. I asked whether they had any idea who might have taken her.

"I was upstairs when I heard a motor coming up the lane," the man said, becoming emotional. "I went to get my glasses and the first thing I saw was two men wearing balaclavas pushing Bertha into the back of a horse box and another one carrying the piglets."

As usual, I started with the Tarot and wasn't too surprised to draw the 'betrayal' card, suggesting that someone in their family had taken the pigs. But the next card was puzzling, the 'justice' card, which only comes out when justice has been done.

"That's wrong," said the lady. "It's us who have lost Bertha."

I explained that the card meant that something was out of balance, and wondered what sort of justice they really wanted – and what had brought them to me rather than reporting the theft to the police? This card can also refer to legal matters, so possibly it would take a court case to get Bertha back. At this point they looked at one another and I felt there was something underlying here that they were keeping secret.

The next card clearly indicated to me an impulsive male who had been looking at the family situation with envy. When I asked whether they had entered Bertha in a show recently, and was told that they had won whilst their son's pig came fourth, it was all falling into place. Especially when the man said, "We don't talk to him anymore."

Spirit showed me a vision of a wheel, a dark-haired man and a black and white cottage with pig pens attached; there was also a plaque with the name of the farm. I thought my client was risking a heart attack, he was so angry when he confirmed this was their son's farm. He turned to his wife and said, "We have to go there and get Bertha."

They then decided to own up and tell me the full story. They had bought Bertha for their son when he was twelve years-old but he never wanted her, so when he left home he'd told them to keep her. They thought of her as their 'baby' and she even had her own bed in their house. Meanwhile their son now had his own farm and was rearing Pot-belled pigs to show. A couple of months ago he had come round threatening to take Bertha back.

"He's a big strong chap and we're in our seventies so we were frightened. I called the police but they said it was just a domestic incident and there were no charges. When we won the show with Bertha, he was furious."

Just then I was given the name 'Humphrey' and they confirmed this was their son. "Well, he's the one who has Bertha and her piglets. I can see money being exchanged too, so you'd better be quick in calling the police or they will have gone to someone else."

The gentleman told me the next day that everything I'd been able to say to them had been right. But they had Bertha and her piglets back now. "We will never talk to him ever again," he said, "and I've cut him out of my Will."

Justice had been done.

One of the best parts of my job is being able to give comfort to those whose pets have passed over the Rainbow Bridge and to reassure them that their animals are now happy and free of pain. It is even better when Spirit shows me some extra information that brings joy to their lives.

A tearful young man came to see me, very emotional about his beloved dog Basil whom he had rescued from Romania.

"I bet you think I'm daft, don't you," he said, "crying over a dog?" I could certainly reassure him on that score. He continued, "I've come to see you because I feel so guilty about having Basil put to sleep. But his legs had given way and then we discovered he had a brain tumour."

As we started the reading, the most beautiful, dignified Akita came forward and telepathically said to me, 'I was loved and I loved them. They gave me the best years of my life, they wrapped me in a blue blanket with my rabbit.' I relayed this message to the young man, who said, "Yes, that's true. We bought him a toy rabbit and my wife filled it with lavender to calm him because he was very distressed when we adopted him. He slept with the rabbit and never once tried to destroy it."

His eyes filled with tears as he began to tell me about the horrendous life Basil had endured before he was rescued. It upset me to hear about the abuse, but this man felt he had to tell me, to justify why he was crying.

"We have no children," he went on, "and my wife had cancer,

so the treatment destroyed any hope of having a family of our own. I work from home and Basil would sit at my feet. We'd even lie down together on the bed when my wife was out. We both genuinely loved Basil and thought we'd done the best thing in having him put to sleep, rather than keeping him alive to suffer further. Does he forgive us?"

I was shown a vision of a slim, blonde woman with a rounded belly and asked the man to describe his wife. He looked stunned and wondered why on Earth I would want to know about her, but confirmed that she was slim and blonde although she had put on weight in the past few months.

"Your wife is pregnant," I told him.

"No, sorry, you're wrong. The doctors said she couldn't have children after the cancer treatment."

"Okay," I replied, "then maybe it's someone in your close family. But I still believe it's your wife. This lady has a small tattoo of angel wings on her arm."

"Yes, it's her," he said, stunned.

I was then able to tell him many things about Basil, the baby they never had, and he left feeling better if rather confused. The following day he called to say that the reason his wife had put on weight was because she was six months pregnant! He said, "How the heck did you know when we didn't?"

A few months later I was out shopping when someone tapped me on the shoulder – it was this young man and his wife with their baby boy. But sadly, not all pet owners are so loving, or even pleased when the story ends well.

A lady called me to say she had lost her dog, Harry, a Labradoodle. She had left a gate open and he'd seen his chance, dashing through it and then vanishing. She insisted that she'd done everything to find him, putting posters up and even employing 'animal finders' at great cost but there was still no news of him.

"Do you think someone picked him up?" she asked. "I've offered a five hundred pounds reward for information. He cost over a thousand pounds when I bought him and he's already sired two lots of puppies."

Harry had been missing for eight days. I'm not familiar with the breed so asked her to describe him: a kind of beige with a lot of curly hair, and chipped. Somehow I knew this was going to a tough one and I didn't yet know whether someone had him or he was merely lost, so I told her I would do my best and be in touch.

"Why can't you tell me now?" she insisted, clearly uptight. I told her I would have to do a ritual and a meditation and then use my pendulum to try and locate the dog. Finding lost pets takes a lot of spiritual energy and people do not realise how draining something like this is, along with the weight of responsibility.

That night I protected myself and called on Black Feather to help me find Harry. What I was shown shocked me. I saw a stone-built house, detached and in the middle of nowhere with high fencing all the way around the garden. As I went deeper into meditation, I saw a dog but he was shaved, he had a wound on his shoulder and another on his abdomen where he had been castrated. But he was wrapped in a pink blanket and wore a pink collar which confused me – was I getting mixed up? Then I was given the name 'Shari'.

As I delved deeper, I saw a signpost at a place about twenty miles from where Harry had disappeared. So when I came out of the meditation, I got out a map of the region and used my pendulum over the area I had seen in my meditation. The pendulum's swing soon confirmed to me that Harry was there. Now the hard part – I had to 'phone the lady back.

"I am sorry to tell you—"

"Is he dead?" she butted in.

"No, he's not dead, but he's been shaved, his chip has been removed, and he's been castrated and he's wearing a pink collar. Oh, and he's being called Shari."

She screamed and her husband came on the line, saying

that his wife was hysterical and what had I said to upset her? I repeated my message, saying that his wife had asked me to find their dog and I was only telling them what Spirit had given me.

"We bought him to make money," he said. "He's a pedigree." And with that he put the 'phone down.

When I'm asked to find a pet, I never take any money for my work even though it's an exceedingly difficult task. In any case, after that response I did not expect to hear from these people again; I just hoped they would find Harry, or Shari. But the lady did call back two days later to say that they had indeed found the dog where I'd said he was.

"But he's no use to us now he's castrated. Those people found him on a lonely road and decided to keep him. They've given us some money for him so it's all right." And that, as they say, was that.

Gypsy Rose Lee and her husband Tommy were good friends with my mother and her friend Freda, and we often joined them in the fields for pea and potato picking when I was young. I loved Rose, she was tiny and Tommy was a big, gentle man. They lived in the wood across from where we lived. I loved to visit them and all their animals: there were the horses that pulled their caravan, Stan and Jonny, and they had two very noisy Jack Russell dogs, Bella and Silva.

They also had two Mynah birds, Micky and Mabel, who would imitate human sounds and words. They were very funny. When Mam was having her tea leaves read by Rose, for instance, Rose might say, "He is spending all the money at the bookies", but she dare not mention my father's name otherwise Mabel, the cleverer of the two, would call out, "Jack's at the bookies!" We would all laugh and then Mabel would mimic our laughter too. My father never visited Rose and Tommy, though, and they didn't like how he treated me and my Mam.

I loved to listen to the stories Rose and Tommy told of the old days when her mother would take her hawking, making and selling clothes pegs, and even travelling up to north Yorkshire to pick the heather. At Christmastime they would make mistletoe and holly wreaths, taken from the surrounding woods. As a child, I was fascinated by them and thought their way of life would suit me.

One extremely hot day, Tommy put the birds outside for some fresh air and shouted to Rose to watch them while he went to the stream for some water, taking the dogs with him. But when he came back, the cage door was open and the birds had gone. Rose insisted that she'd only left them for a minute and thought someone must have been watching her. She was so distraught she called for my mother to help calm her down.

"We'll find the birds, Rose, don't worry," I said to her. "Let's use your crystal ball."

"What a little gem you are, Emus," she said. Emus was my nickname and I still don't know where it came from. We gathered round while Rose looked into her crystal ball and seemed to go into a trance. "I can see two lads," she said. "One has glasses on, the

21

other has ginger hair. And the one with glasses has his hand bleeding because Mabel's bitten him." I asked her if I could have a look too and she replied, "Of course, it's all part of your spiritual journey."

The crystal ball felt very hot. I gazed into it, not expecting to see anything, but then suddenly saw the colour ginger and a scout penknife. It was quite an unusual one, red with a bird's head on it, and I recognised it at once because I knew the lad who had that knife. I was in the Girl Guides at the time and we'd joined the Scouts one afternoon because some of us were doing tests for awards. So I told Tommy who the boy was and where he lived, and we all set off to the lad's house. As we got close, we could hear Mabel squawking and shouting.

"Where's my dinner, Rose? Bugger off, Tommy!"

The boys had the birds in a shed. Tommy opened the door and we saw both boys were bleeding and Mabel and Micky were shut in a pen. As Tommy began to tell the boys what he thought of them, their father came in behind us.

"What's the craic here, you gypsies coming to my house?" Now, my Mam had a temper and she turned on him, threatening to call the police to his boys, at which he took his belt off and gave the boys a good hiding. Then he apologised to us and Tommy said, "Okay pal, we'll leave it at that." But I saw Rose's face and knew she wouldn't leave it.

The day after, the two boys knocked on the caravan with a basket of food their mother had sent and promised to help Rose and Tommy with fetching water for the animals. Tommy invited them in for a minute while Rose was boiling up some herbs, and she offered them 'one of our special drinks'. Of course, they felt they couldn't refuse.

"Did you enjoy that, boys?" she asked when they'd finished and they nodded quietly. "Shall I tell you what's in it?" she went on. "Frogs' legs and snails with dog urine."

I was sitting on the steps of the caravan laughing as they both ran out holding their bellies, while Micky was squawking, "Bugger off, Carrot Top!" which Tommy had taught him.

In season, even on cold and windy days, we'd have to get up at five o'clock and my Mam would make our sandwiches – jam or dripping – so that we could catch the lorry for the pea pickers. My father usually spent his money on drink and betting, and the picking was easy money so we had little choice. Mam knew the farmer well because they'd been at school together and he was sweet on her – she had beautiful long, black hair and lovely blue eyes – and she'd asked him if we could take Rose and Tommy along. Some local folk objected to gypsies but the farmer would say, "If you're not happy about Rose and Tom, get off the lorry." Then after a hard day's work we would often settle down to a cup of tea while Rose told her tales about ghosts and spirits. One day, she became very quiet, thinking of the past and we got her to tell us what was on her mind.

"Many years before I met Tommy," she said, "I went courting with another lad called Paddy, a big strong boy who worked on the roads with his brothers. My mother called him 'the black-eyed devil' because he had very dark eyes and she'd tell me that his heart was as black as his eyes. He took me to meet his mother who had the same eyes. She wasn't friendly even though we both came from well-known gypsy families.

"They had six dogs and two in particular were mangy things, Rex and Bess, who snuggled up to me. They looked up at me and I could read their thoughts, 'Take us with you, we have no future here.' These dogs were used for catching wildlife and fighting…"

Rose went very quiet with a tear in her eye and Mam held her hand until she was ready to go on.

"My Dadda wouldn't stand for that, the cruelty, so he reported Paddy's family for the dog fighting. They all left the area, though not before they'd beaten Dadda up. But the dogs had gone missing, which really upset me so I asked our patron saints Sarah and Christopher for help. I had a vision of the dogs in the woods and recognised the place because—" she winked at us "—I'd been there with Paddy many times. If my Dadda knew he'd have locked me in. Rules were very strict in our culture back then and even my brothers had to be supervised with their girlfriends.

"So I told Dadda I was going to the stream to fetch water and of course he came with me to make sure I was okay. I was the only girl in the family, his princess. We heard a bark and I knew it was Bess so we went further into the woods. I called out to Bess, then we heard more barking like there were a few of them. We followed the barking and found Rex, Bess and another dog Col tied to a tree by a light rope with a long leash. They had food and water, though, and Dadda said we'd keep them even though Bess was in pup. But where were the other border terriers?

"Well, that night I had a dream where I saw the terriers in a disused hut on a farm about a mile away. So the next day we all set off across the fields heading towards the farm, and there they were, the terriers. We couldn't keep them all but my brother said he'd have them. So it was a happy ending. And Bess gave birth to two pups."

"Did you ever find out what happened to Paddy then?" I asked Rose. I sort of knew there was a bit more to the story. She smiled at me.

"Yes, I did see him again at a fair, years later it was. He was with his wife and six kids, and I was married to Tommy by then. As we passed each other he winked at me and smiled, but my Mam was a canny woman and she missed nothing. She said, 'Lucky escape there, Rose.'

"But, you know, animals never forget. We had our Bess with us and when Paddy and his wife passed by she started to shake and hid behind my legs. She was a lovely dog, our Bess, my favourite. She lived to be fifteen years-old and died in her sleep on my bed."

Tommy and Rose were getting old and eventually they decided to go and live with their daughter on a big estate where they could keep their animals. On moving day, Mam, Freda and I went to see them off.

"I have something for you, Emus," Rose said to me. "Never let it go." She handed me her crystal ball and said, "You'll need this to guide you in the future." Now, I often think of Rose and Tommy and the wonderful life they had, moving from one place to another in their wagon pulled by two beautiful horses, accompanied by two noisy and rather rude birds.

It's true that dogs never forget, even when they've been parted from their owners by death. My husband and I often have an outing to Whitby where I like to sit in the abbey on the lookout for Saint Hilda, the Abbess, while Frank sits outside Saint Mary's church overlooking Whitby and watching the boats coming in. It was one of those days when the weather is cold and sunny, and I was composing a magazine article about crystals and their healing qualities.

I heard a low growl down near my feet. Our Mollie had been passed over a couple of years but she never growled, she was the sweetest, gentle little dog. Still, I could feel her by my side in spirit. How strange, I thought, that she was growling – and then I understood why.

"Buddy! Come here, Buddy!" a lady was shouting as a great big Rottweiler was charging towards me. Another spirit presence appeared beside me and a voice said, 'That's my Buddy, he is looking for me.' The spirit lady looked old, wearing a tweed hat and a matching coat, very posh. Soon the dog was sitting at my feet wagging his tail.

"Buddy, come here. Where are you?" Another lady arrived, out of breath, and said, "He won't do as he's told and he's whining and howling all the time. He's not really my dog. He was my Mum's. She passed over two weeks ago and had asked me to take care of him, but I don't think I can."

The spirit lady was looking at her daughter with a scowl on her face. Then she put her hand on Buddy's head and he stopped howling. The lady smiled and said, "He's taken to you, hasn't he?" I was wondering whether I should tell her that her mother was here when she went on, "It feels like my Mum is here somehow. I have a funny feeling and can smell the Coty perfume she wore." I took a deep breath.

"I hope you don't mind me telling you this… but your Mum is standing next to Buddy. That's why he stopped howling, she put her hand on his head."

"Oh, are you one of those fortune-teller people?" she asked.

"No, I'm not a fortune-teller person, I'm a psychic medium who can channel messages from Spirit."

"Really? I thought they all dressed in long skirts with head-scarves and dangling earrings and carried crystal balls… sorry, you must think me very rude."

"I have a gift from God to help people who are grieving or going through a bad time. I pass messages on from Spirit." Right on cue the spirit lady looked at me and said, 'Buddy will soon be with me', but I didn't feel comfortable about repeating this to the lady just now. She put the dog on his lead, saying she had to 'go and feed the brute', and I watched Buddy walk away. He was limping badly and his aura had changed from a light red to a raging dark red around his lower abdomen and back legs.

For several days after this I felt an overwhelming sorrow for Buddy, knowing that he had a stomach tumour and that it was spreading to his back legs. At least, I thought, he would be with his Mummy in the not-too-distant future. Four weeks later, I was sitting at the harbour when the same lady walked past, on her own. She came over and told me the sad news.

"After I saw you, Buddy began to deteriorate. His back legs just collapsed and he couldn't get up. So we took him to the vet who said he had a tumour as big as a lemon in his stomach and it had spread to his legs. There was nothing they could do for him and the kindest thing was to put him to sleep." She then said that she'd known her mother was there with them because she smelled the same perfume again. And it was if she had called Buddy's name because he lifted his head up and looked straight ahead, and even though he was paralysed he'd wagged his tail.

"I'm happy he's with his Mummy," I said. This started a conversation about where pets go when they die. I explained about angels escorting them to a place called the Rainbow Bridge and about how they are given healing, all overseen by St Francis of Assisi who's in charge of animal welfare. Then, when they are fit and well enough, they rejoin their previous owners if they are in spirit.

"You seem to know a lot about spiritual things," the lady said. "I wonder if you would give us a talk at the Women's Guild?" Well, I had experienced a group of women like that before who were very rude and sceptical, and I don't need to justify myself. I told the lady that I don't live in Whitby and that we were going home the next day, which was true, and didn't know when we would be back.

"Well, I'll watch out for you when the town hosts its next Psychic Fair," she said.

"Of course," I said. "I'll be the one in the corner wearing a long skirt with dangling earrings and holding a crystal ball."

She laughed at last and said, "You weren't going to let me forget that, were you?"

Next time we visited the town I would be sitting in the ruins of Whitby Abbey, people-watching or perhaps talking to the spirits in the graveyard. For today, I was just glad to know that Buddy and his owner were reunited.

My meetings with spirit dogs have not always been so pleasant, though. One lovely sunny day, my daughter and I decided to walk our dogs through the local Anston Stones wood, which was famous for supplying the Royal Navy with some of its 'Hearts of Oak' timber. I feel at home in this place and love walking there, seeing the changes in nature that the seasons bring and all kinds of wildlife, squirrels, mice and birds.

There are lots of different pathways in the wood and today we decided to try a new one. When we'd climbed to the top of a craggy area, near what is called Dead Man's Cave, my Jake started to growl. He stood like a statue, refusing to move. The atmosphere had suddenly become dark and heavy, pretty unnerving, and when we heard rustling in the bushes I quickly put the dogs on their leads.

There was another low growl and that rustling… and from the bushes appeared a massive black dog. It looked supernatural, something like a Rottweiler, with a long body, bloodshot eyes in a flat face with rounded ears, and a long tail. Even I was terrified for once. Then it simply vanished in front of our eyes. It's a well-known local legend, but we had just witnessed for ourselves the Black Ghost Dog of Anston.

We looked around and realised that we were lost. It was getting hotter and the dogs were panting, so I prayed for help to find our way home. After a while we recognised a particular tree that has a weird shape so we knew where we were. Hopefully, the Black Ghost Dog had not followed us – or so we thought. There was a rustling in the bushes again…

3

Dealing with Grief

I wanted to write this book in particular because I know that many readers will be grieving for a lost, much-loved pet, as I have myself. I am privileged to be able to see these special furry spirits through my gift of clairvoyance and to know that, when they have passed over, we can take comfort that they are well cared for in the afterlife. And even then, they often give us little signs that they are still with us. But it's also important that we have some understanding of how to deal with the grief of their passing.

My family has used the Kübler-Ross model[1], which finds that we all suffer from a similar pattern of grief: first denial, then anger, bargaining, depression and finally acceptance. This is a framework that most of us pass through when we have lost someone or, indeed, a beloved animal. In these circumstances, people will ask you, "How are you doing?" and we tend to shrug it off and say, "Okay", because our culture teaches us that we have to stay strong and present a picture to others that we are coping. Inside, however, your heart may be shattered into a

[1]   *On Death and Dying* by Elisabeth Kübler-Ross (Simon & Schuster, 1969)

million pieces as a profound sadness eats away at you, and you're thinking, 'How am I going to get through this? What is expected of me?'

The Kübler-Ross framework teaches us that it's natural to be vulnerable and to experience grief in our own way. In fact, people who talk about their loss tend to heal faster than those who harbour the sadness inside and unspoken. Grief is part of the human condition and passing through its stages will bring an end to the sadness for most of us.

In life, our pets become our companions, best friends and at times our saviours. Yet every pet, like humans, goes through the process of the end of life. Sometimes, people are unaware that their pet may be suffering or, unable to accept that they're losing their friend, they do everything possible to try to extend the animal's life, spending every penny they have.

I know what denial is like. My Mollie was deteriorating for a month and the kind, old-school vet told us that she was extremely ill. But still we could not accept she was dying, even when the vet showed us the x-ray of her heart, so large that it was failing. She started to have fits, which I controlled with Valium. We took her for walks with her companion Jake, our fox terrier, and my daughter's dogs, but it was becoming increasing difficult for her. We did discuss that it was nearly time for her to be put to sleep, but still we hung on with the vet giving her steroids to prolong her life. Eventually, she couldn't walk and I had to carry her to bed, where I would sing to her and stroke her head. My heart was breaking and I knew we had to get out of this denial and accept that she was never going to get better.

Mollie loved her food and when she was well she would eat Jake's too. Finally, one Sunday morning, I cooked her favourite meal because I knew she would die that day but she refused to eat. What made it more distressing was that the other dogs were backing away from her, as if they knew. When she started to cry, we knew the decision had to be made to let her go. I wrapped her in her favourite blanket and took her to the vet, where I whispered in her ear that she was loved and asked her to let me know she was okay.

Jake was utterly lost and kept wandering around, staring into space. A week later, I got up at 3 a.m. – I had a bad stomach and often did this to have a cup of milk and a biscuit with Mollie at my side – and when I was in the kitchen I clearly felt something brushing my leg. It was our little lass come back in spirit, to let me know she was fine. So now we had passed through the first stage of grief.

Mollie was a man's dog. She adored my husband, Frank, and she was his lapdog, totally a Daddy's girl. In the past they would walk for miles every day. But now I was angry that we had kept her alive through our own selfishness, and even angry with the vet whom we had known and trusted for years. I was angry because I had not sought a second opinion, despite having seen the x-ray and knowing she had heart failure. Still, 'what if?' consumed my thoughts, as it would for many people. Then I would think back to her deterioration and be angry that we had not made the decision to have her put to sleep before everything became worse.

The anger has now gone because we took the decision to release her from her pain and illness, and were at peace with that decision. When her spirit appeared to me later, she was bright-eyed and looked really healthy, with a white light across her back.

Before Mollie died, I would pray to the Archangel Fhelyai to help her through the illness and to look after her when she passed over. Fhelyai is the 'angel of animals' and brings a wonderful, yellow healing colour when a pet is ready to pass over. Yet despite my spiritual understanding, later I would keep thinking things like, 'What else could I have done?' 'Would it have made any difference if I had taken her to another vet?' 'Was there a chance to save her?' 'Did I not pray hard enough?' 'Why did spiritual healing not work?' These questions and a hundred others went through my head until at last the bargaining cleared my thoughts and helped me to move on.

It is so important for people to realise that depression is not a sign of mental illness, it is the mind dealing with grief, in this case the loss of a loved one. Nor is there any set time period for this or any other of the stages; it may take months, you may move on to the next stage and still have the depression lingering every time you think of your loss.

Thankfully, for me, this stage did not last long because I was helped by having my other dog, Jake. But I certainly did experience that heavy, hopeless feeling that comes with depression and even Jake himself went through a kind of breakdown: he would not eat, he lay in Mollie's bed and he wandered around crying, looking for her. Still, you go through your normal daily activities until it passes. We still walked every day with my daughter's dogs even though it was heart-breaking at times to see only the three of them chasing each other around the fields.

The normality of life heals and at last we came to accept that nothing could have been done to save Mollie's life. We had spent a lot of money on medical investigations and treatments but this didn't matter. Admittedly it was more difficult for my husband since Mollie had been his girl and part of his daily routine, walking through the woods and meeting up for a chat with his friend who had three dogs. It takes a while, but this stage is about accepting your beloved pet has gone and cannot return in earthly form. It does get easier as time goes by.

However, Mollie has been back in spirit form and, even though she cannot share my milk and biscuits, she still accompanies me in the early hours of the morning. (Later in this book there is more about recognising the signs and communicating with your pet.)

We all have our own ways of coping with such unhappy situations and, for me, one of these is using crystals for healing. For example:

Rose Quartz   This is a beautiful pink crystal that brings peace and acceptance in an emotional situation. It connects to the heart chakra.

Green Aventurine   A wonderful healing stone, also a powerful heart healer that connects us with Archangel Raphael, the Master Healer.

Snowflake Obsidian   This is called 'the stone of change' and helps us with the changes that are coming in life without our beloved pet.

Naturally, before attempting any animal healing the most important thing is to visit your local veterinary practice for a wellness check-up, which could highlight problems that perhaps cannot be helped by healing. Now, I don't profess to be an animal healer yet I do know that when we look into an animal's eyes they will convey to us how they feel. And you don't have to be a qualified healer to be able to help your pet because they will respond to your feelings, emotions and loving intentions. They have a brain pattern that allows them to connect in thought with each other and with us, and they do seem to like spiritual energy.

Like us, animals have their own magnetic field, the aura, which emits a low intensity glow that cannot be seen by the naked eye although, when your animal is ailing, you may well recognise the signs. When you bring the energy of a crystal into your pet's aura it will act as an 'oscillator' or a 'stabiliser'. For instance, the calcium in a crystal will connect with the calcium in the body, helping to strengthen the bones. Placing the master healing crystal clear quartz on your animal's solar plexus will transfer your healing energy to your pet. It can take ten minutes so be patient.

For myself, I always ask healing angels to come forward and help, the archangels Raphael and Gabriel being the ones most called upon, and I visualise their rays of colour surrounding the body, especially green, pink and blue. I also call on my 'power animal spirits' – wolf, bear, owl or tiger, depending on which animal I wish to help. Clearly, if it's a cat I'll call on tiger and owl for a bird, wolf for a dog, whilst bear is a major healer who always comes through and is a great companion for the human doing the healing.

Sadly, though, sometimes our pet cannot be healed but at least we can give them our love and help them to be at peace when they are ready to pass over, so we know we have done our very best to help them. Our hearts may be breaking when we see the deterioration in them with every day that comes. What are the signs to watch out for?

- ✎ A poorly pet will usually distance itself from other pets, preparing to be alone. They may want to walk on their own and will not join in with the other pets.

- ✎ Animals feel vulnerable when their bodies begin to weaken and they don't want other animals to see them in this state. For example, losing control of the bladder and bowels is demeaning and they are ashamed, but they cannot do anything to control this.

- ✎ We may be trying to cuddle them but they shy away from us. It's nothing personal, just the nature of an animal's persona, their instincts.

- ✎ Your furry baby may be old and infirm, so don't chastise them for any little 'accidents', just clean it up. Stay calm because if your pet sees how stressed you are this will cause them pain.

- ✎ Above all, allow your pet to maintain their dignity as they approach the Rainbow Bridge. And when they pass, and you're preparing for cremation or burial, a nice thing to do is to wrap them in their blanket or a familiar jumper of yours.

This is an emotionally charged time for a pet's owner, of course, and these last days are ones that will be remembered clearly. One other issue is that many people, friends and neighbours, struggle with what to say to you. It's not easy, talking about a lost pet, and some people just don't think or know how to express their condolences. You may hear comments like, 'It was their time to

34

go', 'They are in a better place now', 'Time is a great healer' and even 'Are you getting another pet?' People mean well but sometimes the words just come out wrong, so we must try not to get upset by ill-thought comments.

We do find our way through grief eventually. Many people, like myself, prefer to grieve alone; when I lost my dog, several friends sent a consoling text and I was glad they didn't 'phone to discuss it all because my grief was too raw. A few months later, when acceptance had come, I was able to look back at the happy memories my pet brought me.

And after all, remember that your pet loved you unconditionally and would not want you to live your life grieving. You will meet again anyway and, when our own time on Earth has ended, our furry friends will be there to welcome us to the spirit world so we have that to look forward to.

You may be asking how I can be so sure of this… In my work as a clairvoyant medium, the visions I have been shown are proof that pets do return and on many occasions I have felt their fur brushing my leg as though to say, 'I am here and ready to connect.' At times like this, what I sense from an animal is a feeling of peace and bliss. I have always been able to communicate with animals, both alive and deceased.

If a client asks me to connect with an animal, I will call on my guide Black Feather to come forward and make things smoother, and I acknowledge an animal's energy in just the same way that I do with humans, by tuning in to Spirit. Animals who have departed this life are pure energy and easy to connect with, whilst just like us animals each have their own personal energy. When an animal sends a message to their owners, it comes to me telepathically or as a vision that I interpret as best I can. Some clients bring a photograph, which helps the connection, although to be honest I prefer not to be told any information at first because I trust Black Feather totally. He has always been much involved with the animal world and has shown me many visions of his life with animals.

However, every soul needs a period of healing and adjustment after it has completed a life on Earth, and every soul has its own personal journey, so it may be a while until an animal is well enough and able to communicate with you. Please, never think that your pet has forgotten you; it's just that they must be ready to come through the many spiritual dimensions. Spirit communication is not an easy matter!

Our pets' journey to the afterlife is a little different from ours. Who comes for them? If they have human family in spirit, they may see these people but at first it's Archangel Fhelyai, and sometimes Archangel Ariel, who tends to them. Fhelyai has a beautiful yellow healing ray that he shines on all the poorly animals. They are kept warm and comfortable while their health is gently restored, and there are angelic helpers allocated to each animal that passes over[2].

What about abandoned, neglected or feral animals? There are no 'bad' animals, some just need extra healing and they will pass into St Francis of Assisi's care. He is, if you like, a celestial warden giving extra care to the very poorly or neglected ones, along with those pets who have been in great pain through illness.

I was shown the Rainbow Bridge once in a deep meditation after we had lost our Mollie. I saw her sitting with my Mam-in-law, Flora, along with all our other dogs. The place looked so peaceful and bright, with other people holding cats, birds, dogs and a whole range of animals, and I could really feel the love permeate from it. When your pet has had enough of this earthly life, be assured that they will be in the arms of celestial healers and are well cared for.

---

[2]   Please see my book, *The Angels Beside Us* (Local Legend, 2020) for more about the angelic world.

4

Angie's Gift

Soon after Nigel and his young son moved into their new home, he told me, they got a rescue cat through the PDSA as a pet. Angie was a tiny thing, crossbred and about one year-old; she had been abandoned when her mother died and had clearly been through some difficult experiences. She was very wary of people but sweet-natured. From the beginning, it was also clear that she had a very independent mind and preferred the outdoors, definitely not a house cat content to sit on a lap and watch television, and she ignored the toys and comfortable basket bought for her. She would come and go in the garden and beyond, always returning for her food at night, very much a free spirit.

At about four years-old she had a nasty accident, getting caught up in a neighbour's wire netting and losing a lot of blood as she struggled. They got her to the vet just in time and she needed an operation and a lot of aftercare. But following this, she seemed to appreciate humans better and her relationship with Nigel and his son became closer – well, as close as a relationship between a human and an independently minded cat can be!

Angie developed a stomach tumour and died at the age of eighteen in 2014, her ashes being buried in the garden at her favourite resting place. Later, Nigel also put a small stone monument there for her. This was in a wooded area close to where he would sit and meditate each night.

One night in the early summer two years later, he reports, he was there as usual and feeling especially peaceful when his thoughts focused strongly on Angie. So he talked to her in his mind for some time, telling her how much she was loved and missed and recalling her adventures, saying that he even missed the occasional dead mouse she would leave as a 'gift' by the back door, though he hardly approved of that!

Early the next morning, Nigel had an appointment and went out to his car to find a dead mouse right beside the driver's door. Nothing like this had happened since Angie's death and, he says, it hasn't happened since despite there being several other cats in the neighbourhood. He couldn't help thinking that Angie's spirit had somehow influenced one of these other cats to leave him a 'message'.

We may not like this behaviour but we must accept that it's natural for cats, and especially for an outdoor animal like Angie. Nigel says that at first he felt upset to see the mouse, but this turned to happiness with the thought that perhaps Angie's spirit had heard him the night before and was responding.

And there was more. Nigel has studied the paranormal for many years and has written a book about synchronicity – the appearance, if we are mindful, of 'signs' or significant events at important moments. On his car journey that morning, he told me, he then noticed the registration plate of a car that travelled in front of his for a long way: AMO...ANS. Now, 'amo' is Latin for 'I love you' and 'Ans' was an abbreviation Nigel often used in his work to mean 'the answer'.

Elaine told me the story of her three pet dogs in spirit, given through the medium and animal communicator Melanie Cruickshank. The first dog had been Millie, "the really bossy one", followed by Jake and then most recently by Lucy.

Angie

"Jake is talking about how poorly he was at the end," said Melanie, "but that he felt happy and cared for. It was Millie who came for him when he passed to the spirit world. He says he spent his last weekend with people coming to see him. He knew there was someone else due to come but was dithering about whether he could." A surprised Elaine agreed that this was true. Her ex-husband had said he would come but then didn't, and it seems that Jake sensed this. That same day, Jake was put to sleep.

"So as I look down," Melanie went on, "I see myself standing on beautiful spring grass covered with daisies and lying at my feet is Lucy. She is tired but enjoying the sunshine on her face. Now I hear a voice say 'Jake' and he comes to stand over Lucy. You may think it odd, but when I do animal readings they come through in different outfits – Jake is looking smart, wearing a waistcoat and dickie bow!

"He says to me, 'I have got her now and I will take good care of her. When she is ready, we'll walk the rest of the way together.' He shows me in the distance the same image I always see of the place where animals go to when they pass over. For now, he says, he's told her to rest up in this beautiful field of daisies and with the scents of springtime. When she is healed a little more, she will walk with him back home so they can all be together again. And he says, 'I love you'."

Elaine also went to my friend Lisa Ball, another animal communicator, and Jake said that he was with Lucy and Elaine was not to worry. She was very comforted by this and she now has another furry friend at home, a beautiful rescue dog from Spain called Luca.

Sadly, many animals are mistreated and one harrowing example – though with a happier ending – was Brutus. Andrea had rescued Brutus from a man involved in the cruel (and illegal) 'sport' of dog fighting. His ears had been cut off with scissors at two months old, he'd been pumped full of steroids and he had scars all over his body. Unsurprisingly, he was terrified of people at first and he barked constantly, the only way he knew how to communicate.

"Yet he was such a loving boy," says Andrea. "He was mentally challenged because of his early life and I think he still thought of himself as a puppy. But he brought great joy and mischief into our lives."

Andrea's neighbours had mice so they put poison pellets down, but Brutus ate some of them and became extremely sick. She says they would have paid anything to save their 'boy', but the vet told them it wouldn't matter how much they spent, Brutus could not be saved. The vet even had to double the usual dose to put him to sleep because he was such a strong dog.

"I was on bedrest at the time with high blood pressure," Andrea continued. "I was pregnant and at high risk. But then I lost the baby soon after Brutus died and we were totally devastated. It was completely heart-breaking and I was encapsulated in grief. It felt like I had lost two babies in a short period of time.

"Then one night Brutus came through to me in a dream. There was a doorway in a meadow and I could see him on the other side of it. Before I walked through the door, I was consumed with sadness even though I could see him on the other side. But as soon as I walked through that doorway, I was completely at peace and overwhelmed with feelings of love and contentment. Brutus told me he was in a better place now and that we would play together again in another lifetime."

Following this, Andrea came to see me for a reading and I was able to contact Brutus. The first thing I noticed was that he had his ears back. Brutus was then able to give me good 'evidence' that reassured Andrea. For example, he showed me a distinctive silver water bowl that was meaningful, something very characteristic of their relationship: he would have always refused to drink from the bowl if there was even a hair in the water, and would knock it over to let Andrea know! She was forever gently telling him off for this. Now, after such a difficult life, he was at peace.

Sometimes, pets don't need a medium to communicate with their owners left behind in this world. Kim Lomas is a spiritual lady who often meditates and has visions of other worlds, and she told me about her first rescue dog, Noah, whom she found at an animal sanctuary. Noah was the runt of the litter and had been taken there by an old man who owned the mother. The dog was riddled with worms and fleas from birth and nobody wanted him. But Kim took one look at his little face in the sanctuary's nursery and that was that.

"He was able to come home a few weeks later," she said. "They told me, 'Take him, and either he'll survive or he won't!'

"Every morning I would come downstairs not knowing whether he would be dead or alive, but he got stronger each day. They'd said he probably wouldn't grow much but he ended up the size of a donkey. One day when he was fourteen, he suddenly looked old, his eyesight was cloudy and he already had bad arthritis. I knew he didn't have much time left. A few days before he passed over, I took his photo and when it was printed Noah seemed to have a beautiful halo around his head.

"A few days after he left us, I was shown in a vision that he had not realised he was in spirit. I saw an Indian lady in a gold and orange sari who had come to fetch him. She was showing him his earthly body, then the two of them faded away.

"After a couple of weeks, in another vision I saw my Dad standing behind an old chair. Dad smiled and looked down from over the back of the chair and in the chair was Noah. He was fast asleep with his back to me and looking like he was recovering from leaving us.

"There was nothing more," Kim continued, "until the following year, actually on Mothering Sunday. I got a wonderful shock… in this vision, Dad was in the distance in a field of golden wheat, then Noah came right up to me and I felt him touch my nose with his. He was healed. Dad called him back shouting, 'Come on then, lad' and the connection ended."

These were wonderful and reassuring experiences for Kim but perhaps the best was yet to come. Another year passed by until, in the next vision, Noah showed himself to her and shoved a puppy towards her. The words 'new-born' were spoken and the puppy rolled a ball to her. He had the curly poodle hair, a miniature version of Noah, and Kim knew this was to be their next pet.

But where to start to find this puppy? Kim's husband Steve went online to look for rescue dogs. At first there was nothing, then he shouted excitedly that he had found an elderly man whose bitch had had puppies. She was a Jack Russell and the father was an apricot poodle belonging to his daughter, who had left the dog with her parents while she went away. The pair had obviously been unsupervised and, in any case, the Jack Russell was thought to be too old to have puppies.

"Steve 'phoned the man up and we went to look at the puppies," said Kim. "They were all smooth-haired, a few black, a few apricot. I was disappointed because these were not at all like the puppy Noah had shown me. But then the gentleman moved to one side and who should be hiding behind his legs, with a coat of fluffy, curly hair, was the puppy I had seen with Noah. I scooped him up! We called him Caspar, after one of the three Magi who travelled to see Jesus."

Whilst dogs and cats are by far the most popular pets, they are by no means the only animals we like to keep with us. It is estimated that about half of UK adults own a pet, with nearly ten million of these being dogs and just under eleven million being cats. Other kinds of pets are no less beloved – although some of them are far less furry!

During my hospital career I had to do some training in mental health issues, which involved spending time with a Community Psychiatric Nurse. The CPN I was allocated to work with was very laidback and experienced, nothing at all seemed to frazzle him. One day he told me that there were four patients for us to see. What he didn't tell me was that the first patient we were to visit had four pet snakes…

The nurse knocked on the door of his house, which had an American flag pinned to it, and said, "Hello, Mo. Put the snakes away, I have a nurse with me." Then he quietly warned me not to be alarmed by Mo's 'scary appearance'. Well, I'd seen pretty much everything in A&E wards so I was more worried about the snakes than our patient, but all the same I was taken aback when the door opened. Mo was covered in snake tattoos and was wearing a tee-shirt with the logo 'I love the USA' on the front; he looked unkempt and I could smell that he'd been smoking cannabis.

Think about it, a drug addict who keeps snakes, wouldn't anyone be worried? I thought to myself that something awful must have happened in this man's life for him to be like this, and how right I was. The sofa was littered with papers, rollups, paper cups and beer cans so I made a small space for myself to sit down. Then I heard some rustling and looked down to see a snake's head peeking out from under the newspapers; it slithered out and across my lap. I nearly fainted.

"Get it off me," I called out, trying to stay calm.

"Aw ma'am, you're hurting his feelings. He only wants to say hello," Mo said gently.

The nurse asked Mo to put him back in his cage and while he was in the kitchen he told me that Mo lived for his snakes and if he didn't have them he might well commit suicide. As Mo came back in, I looked at him and felt a deep sadness at the life he had endured.

At this moment, a spirit lady appeared to me in the room; she looked Chinese and was smiling as she looked at Mo. I was shown a vision of him in an American military uniform in what looked like a forest with other soldiers, sweat pouring down their faces. I could taste their fear in my mouth and instantly felt a bit ashamed of my own initial anxiety and judgement. Then I saw Mo with numbers tattooed on his underarm. In my ignorance I assumed these were his Army numbers, but I soon realised they were concentration camp numbers for prisoners of war. I asked him why he loved his snakes so much, even having tattoos of them with their names all over his body.

"They saved my life and my sanity, ma'am," he said respectfully. "Would you like to hear the story?"

I said I would love to, just as another snake appeared quietly and settled in my lap. Tentatively, I stroked it to show the animal and its owner that I could be trusted; it was warm and never moved. Mo warned me that his story was shocking so he would make me a coffee to help me settle, and while he was back in the kitchen the nurse whispered to me that it would mean a lot to him to be able tell me about his life. The coffee was extraordinarily strong.

"I put three sugars in it," he said. "It will help."

All the while as Mo talked, the spirit lady spirit was still with us.

"Well, as you can see I'm an American. Have you heard of the Hanoi Hilton, the prisoner of war camp in Vietnam?" I nodded.

"We were captured and put in there, tortured regularly and given, let's say, dirty food. One day I'd had enough and told them exactly what I thought of them, so they hung me upside down for a few days. Then when they cut me down, they put me in a cage with snakes.

"Actually, they did me a favour because I would talk to the snakes and caress them and they slept entwined around me. I was in the cage for a week and I grew to love those snakes. Really, they saved my life – and my sanity." I had a lump in my throat by now. "After we were released," he continued, "I was in hospital for a while and I met my wife there. We came to England and settled here, but she had a stroke six months ago and that's why the house is the mess it is."

I heard the spirit lady say, 'I am waiting for him', and I knew he would be passing over that year. Whether it's a nurse's instinct or a psychic message, I always knew when death would come knocking. Of course, I wasn't going to say anything because Mo already had the look of defeat, but my first thought was what would happen to his pets? To please him, I asked to see the other snakes and he was delighted by the offer, first taking a really big one out of the cage.

"This one is called Yankee, he's my favourite. Here, hold him, ma'am."

I politely declined and admitted that I was scared of him, being so big, so he was returned to the cage. Soon after this we had to leave and when Mo held out his hand to shake mine I felt something like an electric shock, proving my instinct that he didn't have long left. In fact it was only a month later when the CPN called me to say that Mo had been found dead that morning – with all four of his beloved snakes lying beside him. It was sad news but at least I knew he was now at peace with his wife. Whenever I buy candles now, they are the Yankees and I think of Mo, his dignity and his love for his unusual pets.

During my nursing career I worked in several departments and met and admired so many people who go above and beyond to help their patients. The Community Psychiatric Nurses are definitely among these people, often dealing with harrowing situations and abuse, with little reward, yet always with the patience of saints. I thank them for showing me, and teaching me, the humanity of mental health nursing.

Another visit that week was to a mother and daughter who both had mental health problems, each constantly telling the other – as a kind of threat – that they were going to commit suicide. What they perhaps didn't realise is that their parrots Sonny and Cher took everything in.

The nurse told me not to be fooled by these two women because they would be nice to me at first but then soon turn nasty. Things didn't start out like that, though, because the mother came to the door and told us to, well, go away along with a few other choice obscenities. The nurse was completely unfazed by this and got us inside by saying he had brought some chocolates for them.

In the living room were two big cages for two really beautiful parrots. I went up to one of them to say hello and it blurted out, "Julie's taking an overdose, silly —." This was the male parrot, Sonny. The woman shouted at the parrot then told me with no emotion that they were her dead husband's pets; he had committed suicide a year before in this very room. Her daughter now walked into the room completely naked. "She's a lazy —, never gets dressed," her mother told me. The female parrot, Cher, then repeated, "She's a lazy —." It was a sad situation but I was having trouble keeping a straight face.

While the woman put a dressing gown around her daughter, the nurse asked her how she was coping. She said things were hard and that Julie kept teaching the parrots to swear at people. Just then Julie picked up a bottle of tablets, said she was going to taking an overdose and down her throat they went. Her mother was clearly used to this, grabbed her daughter by the hair and put her fingers down the girl's throat. Back came the tablets, only four of them so no danger. This kind of behaviour was not uncommon, it seemed, but the girl refused to go to hospital to be helped so her mother had to look after her. Sonny called out, "Julie's a silly —."

My arm started to tingle, which happens when spirit is near, and then I saw a spirit man who reached out a hand and stroked the girl's cheek. He said, 'Things are changing', and the girl smiled as though she had felt her Dad's touch. To break the tense atmosphere, I went to Cher's cage and said, "You're so pretty" which she repeated back to me. The spirit man was beside me now and both parrots starting squawking loudly.

"They used to do that when Dad was alive," the girl said, calmer now.

I asked her whether she ever went out anywhere with friends and she replied that she wasn't allowed out 'because I am mental'. I told her there were girls her age in hospital who were getting better and making friends, so why didn't she come into the hospital for a week and get to know them. Her mother was scowling at me now and I realised that it was she not wanting her daughter to have friends.

When we left, I felt an overwhelming sadness for this young girl. But about a year later I was out shopping when she rushed up to me and hugged me. She was with her boyfriend who seemed very protective of her. Her mother had collapsed at home and died, and Julie was taken to hospital where she met her boyfriend. They now had a flat together and Julie said she was off all her medications. I asked what had happened to Sonny and Cher.

"They went to a rescue centre until I was well. But then they kept swearing at me and I didn't want them back in my new life so I left them there."

I looked into her eyes and noticed the colour of her face: yes, she had the look of pregnancy that my Grandma Mac had told me about. I didn't want to say too much but suggested to Julie that she might like to get a pregnancy test from the nearby chemist. She bought it, went into the public toilets and came out crying with happiness.

By chance, I was working on the maternity ward when she came in and gave birth to a baby boy.

The parrots Sonny and Cher didn't have the best of homes but usually we do all we can to take care of our pets and give them a good life. Yet sometimes it's the other way round and an animal seems to know that a certain person needs comforting. In my first book[3], I wrote several stories about the ghosts and spirits I encountered while working at the Oakwood Chest Unit. This place was quite rural and isolated and there was a lot of wildlife roaming around. Every morning, our kind domestic lady Peggy would put out bread, birdseed, milk and cat food for them.

One particular pussy was a regular visitor so we called her Peg. The ward had several cubicles and there was a door at each end, so when Peg found an open window or door, she would take the opportunity and be in, strolling along the ward as if she owned it.

Sadly, a lot of the patients here were terminally ill and rarely went home – some nurses called it The Last Stop – so we tried to make it as comfortable and homely as possible. One elderly lady came to us with lung cancer and I was just admitting her when Peg walked past.

"What a beautiful cat," the lady said. "Is she really allowed in the ward?"

"Not officially," I replied, "she's wild and comes and goes as she pleases."

Peg must have overheard the lady complimenting her and decided to look after her! One warm, sunny day, all the patients were sitting out on the veranda chatting when Peg appeared; she had a dead mouse in her mouth and she walked right up to this lady and dropped the mouse at her feet as though to say, 'I have brought you a present.'

"Thank you, Peg," she said. "You're a little star." They seemed to have made a real connection because every day after that Peg would sit at her feet.

One Sunday morning I was on the early shift and the night Sister handed me her report; there had been no change in any of

---

[3]   *Ghosts of the NHS* (Local Legend, 2020)

the patients except that this elderly lady had been poorly during the night. Sister said, "I kept shooing that cat away because she kept whining outside the lady's cubicle."

The first thing I did was to check on all the patients, and when I got to this lady's bedside I found that she had passed over. She had her arms around Peg who was sleeping peacefully there, no doubt comforting her new friend in her last moments.

The relatives were informed and her son told me that his mother had often talked about a cat called Peg and that she loved her. Right on cue, Peg wandered up and sat nearby. I told him that this was Peg and that she was wild.

"I'd like to take her home with me and look after her," he said. "Is that okay?"

I was quite sure his mother would approve of that.

Our pets often become much-loved full members of our families but occasionally they can expose rifts in our relationships. The next story is a very difficult one on a human level but thankfully it has a happy ending – although only just. Vera is an elderly lady who contacted me about her red setter dog, Tessa, who had gone missing while they were staying with Vera's daughter in the Lake District. The lady lived in the Midlands and this was the first holiday she'd had since losing her husband and her other pet, also a red setter, two years before.

Vera was very tearful, saying that Tessa was her soulmate and normally never left her side. The daughter had taken Tessa out with her own two German shepherd dogs. "Her dogs are very unruly. She says that Tessa chased a rabbit and disappeared. I'd told her not to let her off the lead but as always she thinks she knows best."

This relationship was clearly not a happy one and the lady said that she and her daughter were not talking to each other now.

As she described Tessa, I had a clear vision of her – beautiful but wet and shivering, with blood on her legs. I didn't pass this on yet because the lady was upset enough, but I told her that Tessa was still alive and promised to try and find her with the help of her husband. She was shocked.

"You mean you can connect with my husband?" Vera was on an emotional rollercoaster, not knowing what to think or believe. She had put posters up everywhere asking for help in finding Tessa but to no avail and she'd been missing for three days now. She kept saying, "I know she has died, or she would have found her way home to my daughter's place."

I called my spirit guide forward to help and he brought Vera's husband through, along with their other red setter, Tina. The husband showed me Tessa and what had happened to her. She had jumped into a boat with two men but had then fallen into the water and was struggling. The men were wearing green caps with a logo at the front, but I couldn't make it out. They tried to rescue her but then, I saw, she'd made it through the shallows towards the grassy bank and run off into a craggy area.

"Why not take your daughter's two dogs," I suggested to Vera, "and call out Tina's name as well as Tessa's? I'm sure you will find her but be prepared, she's not in a good state. She's limping and has blood on her leg. I think it may be fractured. But someone at the boathouse will know where she is."

After Vera had rung off, I thought I would try again to locate Tessa and I asked Black Feather and Wolf, my spirit animal, for help. I was shown a vision of Tessa sheltering in a cave not far from the boathouse. She had the most beautiful, soulful eyes but they were fading. It looked like she was dying. I rang Vera immediately to tell her what I'd seen and, a few hours later, a very tearful Vera called back.

"We have found her! She was exactly where you said she would be. A man came out of the boathouse and asked if I was the owner of the red setter. He said that he'd been about to go onto the lake with his son when the dog came running up and jumped into their boat. He'd tried to hold her but she scrambled out and ran off.

"Anyway, we found her in a small cave and got her to the vet straight away. He said that if she'd been out another night she would have died."

Vera sent me a photo later of Tessa, alive and well, happily splashing in the water. On a lead!

5

Anita's Baby

In Chapter One I mentioned going to Cruft's to show my fox terrier puppy, Jake. My son Neil came with me and looked after Jake while I wandered round to have a look at everything and watch people grooming their dogs. The hall was buzzing with excited people and animals but somehow I had an overwhelming sense of sadness that I couldn't understand. That is, until I came across the most beautiful black and white Akita with great sadness in her eyes. I asked her what was wrong.

She told me telepathically that she'd had several babies but they had 'all gone'. Her owner was a heavily built, ginger-haired and bearded man who looked like a fearsome Viking. He saw me looking closely at his dog.

"Isn't she a beauty?" he said. "She's my darling."

"You have a very unhappy dog there, mister," I replied. He looked at me accusingly with his head on one side.

"And who are you?"

"I can communicate with animals."

"Oh, you're one of those funny folks, then."

"I am indeed."

"I love Anita with all my heart," he said, "and if there's something wrong with her I want to know. After all, her pups sell for over a thousand." I really didn't think he wouldn't listen to anything I had to say but I was wrong. "They tell me I look fierce," he went on, "but I'm not, honestly."

"Okay then," I said, taking a deep breath, "she's very upset that you take her puppies away from her as soon as they're born."

"Yes, I do take them," he agreed, looking shocked. "And I give her tablets to dry her milk up because I show her all year round – apart from when she's in pup."

"Haven't you noticed that she sits in a corner for days on end after you've taken her babies?"

"You're right there, she won't have anything to do with me. How did I get it so wrong?" He was a bit tearful now but Anita was looking at me intently and wagging her tail.

"Well, have you ever thought of keeping a pup?" I suggested. "That would double your prize money and make Anita happy." He beamed at me.

"We were fated to meet today, thank you," he said.

A year later I was back there again and I looked around for Anita. There she was, looking very happy, and I'm sure she recognised me. She wagged her tail anyway. She was sitting contentedly alongside one of her babies.

It's an inspiring and exciting time when our pets give birth, but our lives can be turned upside down at such moments too. Mrs Jones was admitted to the hospital where I worked for investigations, in particular a bronchoscopy to determine whether she had cancer. She was a very chatty lady and told me that she ran a cattery about a mile away, and she also took in abused and neglected cats. Anyone could tell she was a cat lover because she had cats all over her pyjamas and wore gigantic fluffy slippers with cats' faces on the front.

"I have ten cats now," she said, "as well as my own girl, Masie, who's having kittens soon. She's a snow white. I need to be home before she gives birth because she'll be distraught if I'm not there for her."

Jake

But I was thinking to myself that this lady didn't look too good and I would be surprised if she got the all-clear. She had that murky brown-red aura that I dread and the scent of death was lingering around her. Sure enough, it was bad news – she had lung cancer with metastases in her liver.

Two days later, we heard cats fighting and hissing at each other and I looked through the window to see three of them, two ginger and a beautiful snow white who was obviously pregnant. How on Earth had that cat found where her mistress was? I went outside to pick her up and asked one of my colleagues to lock the outer door in case the Nursing Officer came over; they rarely did but I wasn't taking any chances.

Mrs Jones was asleep so I sat in a chair next to the bed. The cat meowed and the lady's eyes shot open. "That's my Masie," she murmured. "I must be dreaming." When she turned to look at me her face was a real picture. I spread a fresh sheet over the bed and put Masie down with her Mummy, then 'phoned her husband to tell him that the cat was here with his wife.

"Thank goodness," he said, "I thought someone had stolen her. The ginger has gone missing as well – he's the father of the kittens." I told him that, yes, there was a ginger outside who wouldn't go away and Mr Jones said he was on his way now.

That wasn't the only thing on its way because it soon became obvious that Masie was ready to give birth. I found a large cardboard box, lined it with some padding and put Masie in it, whereupon Mrs Jones jumped out of bed and started delivering the kittens. It was like a TV comedy show and I could hardly believe it was happening, just glad that there were a few of us on duty that evening so I could keep an eye on Mrs Jones and her new family.

The cubicle door opened and I held my breath, worried that it was the Nursing Officer and my job was at risk. Sometimes the heart rules the head but surely, on this occasion, it was the right thing to do? Thankfully, it was Mr Jones and he walked in just as the first of four kittens was born. Later, he took them home along with Masie and the ginger father.

"God made this happen, nurse," Mrs Jones said. It was certainly pretty paranormal. One of my colleagues thought the whole thing was really funny and suggested taking the kittens over to the Maternity Ward. The lady smiled and went on, "I know I'm dying but it was my dearest wish that I could deliver Masie's babies. You've made that happen for me and I'll be eternally grateful."

It seems that Masie was not only a very loving and brave cat, but quite possibly clairvoyant too. The following day, Mr Jones brought her in a cat basket to see his wife. They were sitting outside the cubicle chatting when Mrs Jones suddenly just keeled over. A nurse was nearby and caught her, and we got her onto her bed; but her breathing was shallow and she was dying. By the time a doctor got to the ward it was too late.

A couple of weeks later, her husband came back to the ward bringing us some chocolates and to tell us that Masie herself had passed over two days after his wife, although the kittens were all doing well. He was going to sell the cattery because he couldn't cope without his wife, so he was moving on. How sad was that? A few days ago they were planning the future, making the cattery bigger to take in more rescues. But now his heart was broken and the future plans in pieces.

For myself, however, there would always be the memory of an extraordinarily caring, courageous and psychic snow white furry spirit. And I came across another psychic cat with a very individual way of communicating, who not only saved a life but brought about a happy-ever-after…

An elderly lady rang asking me to go to her house to give her a reading. I hesitated at first because it was in the middle of nowhere and miles from where I live, but something told me this was important. As I arrived, five cats came running out of the door. It was a very large house and the grounds were extensive too, with stone statues of Adonis, Venus, cherubs and a massive angel with outstretched wings. Sitting on top of one of the statues, watching me closely, was a ginger tomcat called Melvin.

The lady had limited mobility and I wondered how she coped out here in the middle of nowhere with all these cats; she also told me that she had a daughter who had learning difficulties. "I am eighty-five," she said, "and I had Miranda when I was forty-five – a big mistake. She's uncontrollable and some people want to put her away. But I promised my husband I would never do that."

As we started the reading I got the impression she really just wanted to chat because she was very lonely. She'd had a very privileged life, living in several different countries. At one point, she got up to fetch something and then offered me a gold and emerald bracelet in gratitude for my coming out to see her. But I wasn't going to take that from her so I told a little white lie, saying that I was allergic to gold.

All the while, the cats kept jumping on my knees – except for Melvin who was staring and hissing at me. It was uncanny. Then he looked in my eyes and in my mind I heard him say, 'Danger!' Then I 'saw' the girl's face. Not sure yet what to make of this, we carried on with the reading but then heard screaming outside and immediately I was given a vision of a girl in water. I asked the lady where Miranda was.

"Oh, she's running around the estate, screaming and laughing with the gardener," she said.

"No," I replied, "your daughter is in trouble."

And with that, Melvin's hissing got louder and he ran to the door. I followed him and saw a man with a garden fork in his hand shouting at the girl who was in the river, "Stop being silly, Miranda, I do love you." He saw me running up to him and asked, "Who the hell are you?"

I said I was a friend of the old lady and that Miranda wasn't being silly, she was in trouble. He then waded in to rescue the girl, who was going deeper into the water with her foot caught in the reeds. Next thing we knew, he was under the water too, but he manged to get hold of her. The old lady had hobbled down to the riverside and I said I would call an ambulance but she stopped me. "No, please don't, they will only take her away from me."

As the gardener reached the bank, Melvin attacked him and scratched the poor chap's arm, then jumped into the girl's arms and refused to move, all the while hissing and spitting at the gardener. The situation was becoming most bizarre. Probably feeling unappreciated, the gardener finally managed to pull Melvin off

Miranda by the scruff of his neck and was about to throw him in the water until I stopped him.

"I'm fed up of this mangy cat," he said. "Even when I put my arm around her it scratches and hisses at me." I told him that the cat had saved her life. "No, it was me who saved her life," he retorted.

By now, the old lady had realised what was going on. "Get in the house, you little hussy," she shouted. "I don't know, fraternising with the gardener." I suggested that I could come back another time if she preferred but she said, "No, you won't come back so let's carry on. Cook can look after Miranda."

We settled back down again and soon the lady's husband came through saying, 'Let her go.' The lady shook her head.

"I have cancer," she told me, "and I know I haven't long left. But I don't know what to do about Miranda." I commented that the gardener clearly loved her daughter, and she replied, "Well, what does my husband say? Jonny, will you be waiting for me? And what should I do about Miranda?"

'Let her go,' he said again, 'and make provisions for her soon.'

She seemed content with that. Just then, Miranda and Melvin came into the room and the cat jumped out of her arms onto my knee. I thought he was going to bite me but instead he licked my hand and started to purr. I asked Miranda if she was okay now.

"Yes, and I know he loves me now, risking his life to save me."

"My dear, if you love him and he will look after you, I am fine with that," said her mother. Miranda squealed with delight, wrapped her arms around her Mum and kissed her. The lady said to me later, "She has never done that before."

The lady died six months later and Miranda married her gardener. Melvin was probably the Best Man. I had really hesitated about travelling so far for that reading but now I'm glad I did, because it could have turned out to be a very sad story. And I often think about this clever cat, despite his hissing at me. At least he got my attention and was able to warn me about his mistress being in danger.

Another time, I met some dogs who also absolutely knew what was going on. I had been seconded to do a leg ulcer course, working with the District Nurse, Bridget, and we started in her office at a doctor's surgery, going through the competencies I had to pass in order to be able to redress ulcers. I had my tongue in my cheek and was keeping quiet because I already did most of this work in my regular hospital work. In fact, I had been teaching it to students!

Our first patient was a man with kidney failure and prostate cancer, and I knew as soon as I walked into his room that his time on Earth was limited because he had an aura of pale green and grey. He had three ulcers and a serious pressure sore on his sacrum. The scent hit me straight away, those white lilies that are associated with death.

He was lying on the bed with three dogs. Winston, a Jack Russell, had his head resting on one of the ulcers; Wallace, a female Jack Russell, had her head on the other leg; and a cute little terrier was curled up into his back. They clearly knew what the gentleman's problems were. Then they started barking at us and Winston was snarling; I'm sure they knew their master was dying and thought they were protecting him from us. I asked Bridget how we were going to redress these well-guarded ulcers. She tapped the side of her nose.

"I was a Girl Guide back in Ireland," she said, "and I was taught always to be prepared. When they come to me, slip their leads on and take them downstairs to the kitchen. Close the door or, if you're feeling fit, take them for a little walk while I sit and talk with our patient." Then she pulled out a paper bag, rattled it and called to the dogs, "Sausages!"

I did as she suggested and it only took around ten minutes. The nurse had waited for me, perhaps thinking she would surprise me with what was coming. The dogs were barking and howling downstairs as we first dealt with the pressure sore, then Bridget said, "Right, you take the dressing off the right leg and I'll do the left." The ulcer was covered with maggots – yes, that's right – and

Bridget smiled at me. "I thought I'd surprise you." I didn't have the heart to tell her I redressed leg ulcers and applied these sterile maggots nearly every day[4] at the hospital.

The gentleman's pallor was poor and his lips were blue. I felt so sorry for him, having to cope with all this. It took us around an hour and half to redress his wounds, wash him and make him comfortable, all the while the dogs continuing to howl and bark, scratching at the door. I wondered whether he should go to hospital, which would mean leaving his dogs.

"I am staying with my furry friends," he insisted. "They keep me going."

I let the dogs out and they flew upstairs, at first taking up the same positions as before. Then they all sat up, sniffing the air, before jumping off the bed and cowering in the corner of the bedroom. I thought to myself, 'They've picked up the scent of death.' I had read somewhere that pets distance themselves from their owners when death is imminent, but the gentleman became upset.

"Why won't they come to me?" he cried. Bridget did her magic trick with the paper bag of 'sausages' again and gave it to him to try. It worked.

Many people and animals can recognise the scent of death. Our bodies omit a distinctive smell at this time; to me it's usually white lilies and some of the other fragrances of death are not unpleasant, such as the central nervous system depressant Butanol and the aldehyde Hexanal, which has the scent of newly cut grass. But my belief is that animals have a paranormal intuition of when death is near.

A short while later, the office got a 'phone call from our patient's wife to say that he had died but the dogs would not leave his body – what should she do? Bridget replied, "We'll be with you shortly, I just have to call at a shop first." I smiled, knowing that she was going to buy sausages.

---

[4]   Napoleon's surgeon, Baron Dominique Jean Larrey, discovered in the 19th century that certain flies consume dead tissue and help wounds heal. Their maggots debride the wound.

We did the last offices for him, being very respectful and not talking, to preserve the dignity of the situation, and the dogs sat quietly with his wife. Just as the doctor was going through the legal matters, the lady screamed because the dogs had pulled her husband's pyjamas out of the wash basket and were tearing them to shreds. Winston had the pyjama top in his dog bed and was lying on it. These beloved pets knew exactly what was going on and were carrying out their own last offices.

My secondment ended and Bridget signed me off, having passed the competencies so that I could work on my own doing leg ulcers. Only then did she wink at me and confess, "I knew all along who you were. I was there when you gave a lecture about using maggots on wounds and that surgeon walked out saying, 'We will never use maggots in this hospital.'"[5]

Bridget and I came across an even bigger menagerie another day that week. "Don't look too horrified when you see the next patient," she said as we made our way there. Well, I have to say that nothing shocks me anymore after years working in A&E, so I was just curious about seeing this lady. The door key was left under a heavy, full dustbin which took the two of us to lift; I suppose a burglar would never bother to find it there.

What a surprise I had. The house stank of cats' pee and as we opened the door six cats flew out followed by four dogs – and a pig. Connie was lying on her bed, all thirty stones of her.

"Hello, lovely ladies," she said, then called to her skinny husband, John, "Make the nurses a coffee." I felt a bit sick. The carpets and furniture were filthy with cat litter and droppings, even more cats, and dog poo. I gulped and muttered that I didn't drink coffee, thanks, but John brought me tea anyway in a beautiful China cup. My Grandma Mac's words came back to me: "It's not your right to judge."

---

[5] This is a story in my book *Ghosts of the NHS*. I later gave that surgeon a very evidential message from his deceased mother and his whole personality then changed. From having been something of a tyrant, after that everyone wanted to work with him.

"Sit down, nurses," said Connie, "if you can find somewhere. Just chuck the dog on the floor."

"Um, you have a lot of pets here," I said. "What other animals do you have and do they all have names?" Wrong question. She reeled off about twenty names of pigs, goats, birds, chickens and rabbits apart from the cats and dogs.

Connie had bilateral leg ulcers and was also suffering from a brain tumour. Her husband clearly loved her very much and kept fussing over her, straightening the bedclothes while we started to unwind her bandages. She shouted at him, "Stop fussing, John. Go and feed the horses." When he'd gone she became very quiet and I could see by her aura that she was desperately ill, even though she was putting on a brave front. She looked at me and smiled as out of nowhere four cats and three dogs raced into the bedroom and jumped onto the bed (thankfully, a massive king-size).

Then I heard a voice in my mind say, 'She is going to die soon.' Indeed, the leg ulcers were the worst I had ever seen. We had finished redressing them and she said, "I'm not feeling well but I'm scared of dying. Will you sit with me a while?" We agreed that I would stay while Bridget went on to our next patient and John brought me another cuppa.

I was just chatting away with Connie when all of a sudden two of the dogs jumped off the bed whimpering and ran outside howling. Then the two gorgeous Ragdoll cats started hissing and also jumped off the bed. Connie called them by name but they wouldn't come back. Again, this was the behaviour that animals exhibit when faced with death.

"They know I'm dying," Connie sighed. "The cats are my babies, Cindy and Coco. They sleep with me, never leave me." Connie's colour started to change now so I checked her blood pressure and pulse; her breathing was becoming shallow too and I called to John to 'phone the doctor and ask Bridget to come back. The dogs were howling outside.

As I held Connie's hand I felt a presence beside us and looked round to see a spirit lady standing there, looking down at Connie. She said, 'I have come for my daughter.'

"I know I'm going, nurse," Connie whispered. "Actually, it's a relief. Please tell John he must have my babies put to sleep, I want them with me." This was difficult for me – here were two beautiful Ragdolls and surely someone would love them, but then this was her last wish. She opened her eyes and said, "I can see all my other cats that have died. They've come to be with me. Do you think I'm soft in the head, nurse?" I squeezed her hand and reassured her. "You understand, don't you?" she whispered as she closed her eyes again.

I fetched John and left them together while we waited for the doctor and Bridget to arrive. Soon, John came out of the bedroom and said, "She's gone, the love of my life. You know, she never said 'I love you' in thirty years of marriage, but she said the words just now before she died." Then the commotion started as the cats were hissing and the dogs howling, scratching at the door to get to Connie.

We left John with his wife for a while before going back to do her last offices. It was eerily quiet as we walked in; Connie looked very peaceful and four dogs and six cats were lying beside her on the bed. With a heavy heart I told John what Connie had said about the Ragdoll cats, and was surprised and relieved by his reply. It turned out that Cindy had a tumour in her ear and Coco had leukaemia, so putting them to sleep was the right thing to do.

I met John again in a supermarket some time later and he said that all the pets had been rehomed and he was now moving to Spain to work with an organisation that rescued dogs and cats. I said, "Connie would be proud of you."

"Well, that's why we had so many animals," he said. "It's what she did, rescuing them." He paused for a moment and then asked, "Do you believe in life after death, nurse? Only, she had been saying that her Mam came to see her." I was certainly able to reassure him about that.

Connie's domestic zoo was matched by another one in Australia. Thanks to social media, I am sometimes contacted by people in different far off countries, and Amy got in touch to say that three of her cats had gone missing. All three were males that had not been neutered. They would often wander off looking for girlfriends and always came back after a few days, but it had now been ten days and Amy was worried that something bad might have happened to them. She lived on an isolated farm with ten other cats, five dogs, three goats, rabbits and pigs.

She confessed that she had recently split up with her husband because she'd had an affair with the owner of the nursing home where she worked. She would take these particular cats, Barny, Bertie and Barry, to work with her for the residents to cuddle and at times left the cats there all night so they had the run of the place. Could I find them, dead or alive?

I did my usual meditation and managed to pinpoint where Amy lived, beside a large lake with a wooded area, but I felt the cats weren't around there. What I did feel was their energies so I knew they were definitely in spirit. It was going to be a difficult task for me to find these cats so I called in my spirit guide, Black Feather.

He showed me a man with a black beard, wearing a cap turned the wrong way round and a red check shirt. The man was carrying a spade. Then I saw an area behind the nursing home where there was newly dug soil. I could now see the cats in spirit but still had to understand fully what I had been shown before telling Amy. So I got out my citrine pendulum and found a map of the area.

"Are the cats in spirit?" The answer was 'yes'. "Has the man in the red check shirt killed them?" The answer was 'no'! This confused me for a bit but then I saw another man with a wheelbarrow and a fork, the gardener at the home. "Did the gardener killed the cats?" This time it was 'yes' so I had the culprit. But why had I seen Amy's husband with a spade, then? Aha, then I was shown Amy's husband digging up the cats and putting them in a bag.

I relayed all this to Amy and she confronted the gardener. He admitted the crime, saying he was fed up of putting his hands into the cats' 'muck' so that's why he got rid of them. A little while later her husband turned up with the cats in a bag because, he said, he knew that Amy loved them and would want them buried in her garden.

It was a sad and difficult story. But then Amy emailed me after a couple of months to say that she was reunited with her husband and they were having a baby. There was more. She had adopted three more cats and named one Amy after me (not after herself)!

6

Communicate With Your Pet

Learning the language of animals is a wonderful thing to do. With practice and some spiritual awareness, your pet really can be your best friend. Our pets have thoughts and experience emotions just like we do, and of course the biggest difference between us is the use of language. Yet they communicate with us all the time, expressing their feelings of anger, sadness and happiness. When an animal expresses something, that message is formed by energetic impressions that we can receive telepathically or in a vision.

They also show their thoughts and feelings vocally and through body language, from pricked-up ears, to sniffing and nuzzling up to us or even kissing. I have found that my own dogs each had their own way of communicating. They give off signs in their overall posture, helping us to know what their mood is. A happy dog, for example, is relaxed in body and has a wagging tail; indeed, dogs' tails play a big part in telling us what they are feeling. If the animal is relaxed the tail hangs down, but if it is feeling anxious then it is tucked under its butt whilst the happier the dog is the faster the tail wags. Moreover, with all the dogs I have owned or known through my psychic readings, I have found that I could tell how they were feeling by looking directly into their eyes.

These comments don't apply to every animal, of course. If a cat's tail is wagging it's a sign that they are annoyed. And one should not look directly into a horse's eyes until a good relationship has been established because they may see this as a threat. You may like to refer to one of the many good books written about animal body language; here, we are focusing on psychic communication.

Psychic animal communication is natural. Anyone can talk to an animal, aloud or mentally, and know that they will listen – even if they don't always do as they're told! They receive information and understand our intentions energetically, in the form of thoughts, ideas and images, and sensations in their bodies. And in return, they can express themselves to us telepathically. Whilst the actual mechanism for this is unknown, various scientific investigations have shown that their thoughts and emotions are very real and can be passed on in this way from animals to humans. This can be invaluable in many situations, enhancing shared knowledge and a mental understanding between species. Obvious examples are guide and medical diagnostic dogs, but everyone can learn to communicate with their pet.

I am grateful to the wonderful animal communicator Janine Wilbraham for permission to quote from her book here[6]. This section relates to horses but many of the same principles can be applied with other animals.

"Horses are very spiritual animals and their energy is powerful. This can be badly misunderstood and what people do not realise is that horses can 'read' them the minute they meet. They can

---

6 *Can You Hear Me?* by Janine Wilbraham (Local Legend Publishing, 2011)

read our aura (the aura is a living energy field that surrounds everything and everyone) and tell what mood we are in – happy, sad, nervous or angry.

"If the horse comes to me, I stand outside [their stable] and read their aura. I send them love from my heart and the horse usually comes over. I offer my hand palm down to them, never forcing my hand into their space. I do not scratch their withers or neck because I have not been given permission to do so. I regulate my breathing so the horses can tune into me and feel calm. Only then do I enter the stable. When the animal has given me permission, I start to communicate with them, asking, 'What do you want to tell me?'

"The information I get back does not always come in words, it comes in colours, shapes, symbols, feelings and pictures. Usually, the owner has questions they want answered so I ask those and relay back to the owner what the animal said. Sometimes they do not want to answer questions, so I leave it until later and come back to it, asking in a different way.

"Animals do not talk like we do, they have stilted-type sentences although some can be good talkers. But for me it does not matter whether I have a horse or other animal there in front of me, or just a picture of them: as a natural-born clairvoyant I find this comes easy.

"When a horse gives me colours it can be connected to the horse's chakras and… I will put my hand on the area it is representing. For example, if a red colour is given the animal might be having trouble in their base or root chakra (in a horse this is at the top of its tail). Usually, horses with these problems are quite fearful. In brief, the seven main chakras of the body are:

- 🐾 base: red
- 🐾 sacral: orange
- 🐾 solar plexus: yellow
- 🐾 heart: green

- throat: blue
- third eye: indigo
- crown: violet.

If [an animal] has pain it shows up in my body. Moving on to distance healing, communication is done by spiritual energy."

Indeed, I have often been able to use colour in seeing that an animal is unwell but in my case it's by observing the colours of their auras. We all have an instinct of danger, perhaps feeling particularly uneasy in an unfamiliar place or finding the hairs on our necks stick up for no obvious reason. This is the aura reacting to the surrounding energy.

When I am walking my dog, I can tell if another person's dog is friendly or not, or if it is ill. One day I came across a lady whose dog was limping and I asked her whether the dog had hurt its foot. At first she was very defensive and said, "Do you think I'm abusing him?"

"Of course not," I replied, "it's just that… can you check his left paw?" She lifted the paw up and there was a raw area that looked like a tumour. She asked me how I'd known but I just suggested she get him to the vet as soon as possible and reassured her that he would be okay. I had seen the aura of the dog's left leg was an angry red and, in the middle, pale green, which is how I knew he would be fine once the tumour had been removed. I saw the lady again about two months later and she ran up to me.

"I took our dog to vet and you were right," she said. "She had the tumour removed and it's okay now. I hadn't thought to look under her paw, so thank you."

When I go to the vet's surgery myself, it's hard seeing so many poorly animals. One day a lady came in with a huge black rabbit. I could see into his cage and his aura was a dark green; I also noticed a red area around his stomach with spots of green in it and knew immediately that he was allergic to the hay he was lying on and nibbling at. When the lady came out of the surgery she was clutching some medication to help with his stomach problem, and as I left I found her still sitting outside, very upset. I asked her what was wrong.

"The vet says he needs a gastroscopy," she said. "It's going to be two hundred quid altogether."

"I noticed his hay was a bit dark. Why don't you try wood shavings?" I suggested. "Your rabbit won't eat them so it might help him."

A while later I ran into her again at the surgery and she said she was glad she'd met me; she'd got some wood shavings for her pet's cage and he started improving straightaway. I looked into the cage and saw a beautiful pink and green aura.

I have always been able to see auras and many people have found that they can learn this skill. We should not assume, however, that we can diagnose illness by their colours, and what I see and interpret is probably different to what others might see because of my long personal experience. This is what I have found:

- ❧ Purple   I feel privileged if I see a purple aura because it is a very spiritual colour, the highest in the aura spectrum. This colour symbolises high morals and an ability to connect with animal spirits.

- ❧ White   Not a common aura colour but also very spiritual.

- ❧ Blue   All depends on the shade of this colour. For instance, a deep blue shows unhappiness and if I see this in the aura of an animal I know that the animal is insecure and may bite.

- ❧ Pink   This is the colour I want to see in an animal's aura. It means that this animal is loving and gentle, loves to make friends and has a beautiful soul.

🐾 Green   The colour of healing. The lighter the green, the more likely it is that this could be a therapy animal. If the aura is an emerald green, the animal is healing from some trauma.

🐾 Red   I don't like to see this colour because it means anger, illness or danger. This animal is in distress.

My own daughter contacted Janine Wilbraham for help with her horse, who is an Irish Draught, a big boy at seventeen hands. Karen has always had horses since she was little and there have been so many, all chestnut and usually thoroughbred. She had been without a horse for a year when her husband said he would buy her one for her birthday. She asked me to look into my crystal ball to find her the right one; naturally, she wanted a chestnut thoroughbred. But I told her that a white horse was coming into her life, he was from Ireland and had not been treated well.

"You're wrong, Mum, I would never have a white horse," she said. I just shrugged my shoulders and thought, 'Let's wait and see.'

A week later, she saw a horse that she wanted advertised so they went along to see it. As they pulled into the yard, two horses had their heads out of the stable doors, the chestnut and a white one. The white one looked her right in the eye and whinnied as though to say, 'Here I am, take me home!' Karen looked at her husband astonished and said, "My Mum was right again."

The horse had no name, only a passport, so she called to tell us what had happened and said, "Write down on a piece of paper what you think we should call him." She did the same. Later, we exchanged papers and had both written 'Gabriel'. But we knew almost nothing about the horse's background.

One day, she was out riding him when he was startled by a bird flying in front of him and reared up, throwing Karen. As she lay on the ground unconscious, Gabriel kept nudging her and whinnying to attract someone's attention. She was admitted to hospital with seven cracked ribs, a punctured lung and a spinal fracture, from which she has now fortunately recovered. But she was concerned that something may be wrong with Gabriel so she asked Janine to do a reading and try to discover what the problem was with him.

"Gabriel had been cruelly treated when he was in Ireland," she told us. "He was passed around to so many people he felt unloved. Now he has pain in his stomach…" She was right, it turned out he had stomach ulcers. Then he also told Janine that he had found his 'forever home' and loved his new owner.

Gabriel

I believe wholeheartedly that if your pet wants to communicate with you it will find a way, and I have already shared some stories of when they have come through at psychic readings, or even when I'm not expecting it. Usually at such times, the animal is accompanied by a human loved one who has also passed over, they rarely appear on their own.

Naturally, receiving a message from your pet can be quite emotional and, indeed, unexpected. When I am asked for a reading, I first make sure that I and my client are psychically safe by adding protection to us and the room. There are, I'm afraid, 'mischievous entities' that sometimes try to slide in and give false messages. At such times, the client is emotionally charged and could miss the signs of this so I never take anything for granted, making quite sure it's a genuine connection and any message I pass on is truthful.

When pets are able to come through, they have to pass through many dimensions to be with us; we cannot control this process and cannot make it happen so, when it does, we must enjoy every minute. Be encouraged that there is every chance your pet will come through, alongside a deceased loved one. But trying to force this spiritual connection is not only wrong, it won't work.

"I lost my cat when she was seventeen," one client told me. "She had been run over outside my house by a car that didn't stop and Tina was left at the side of the road in a ditch." The lady was clearly very upset and started to cry, so I waited until she composed herself even though I could feel Tina coming forward. I didn't tell the lady yet because I felt she needed to finish her story. "She was in the ditch for two days. She had a bell and a cat-shaped name tag, but when I found her they were missing. I was so distressed, suicidal."

She went on to say that she was feeling guilty and needed forgiveness. I wasn't sure why. But what she said next shocked me: she had already seen five other mediums in a week, trying to get them to bring Tina forward. They had all said, "It's not your fault", but she hadn't felt any genuine connection – and she had a certain question that none of them could answer.

I had to be straight with her and say that if Tina wasn't ready to come forward, then no matter how good a medium is they will not be able to bring her through. Then I braced myself and asked, "Okay, what's the question?"

As soon as I spoke, a spirit lady appeared beside us holding Tina, saying, 'Tina is buried with me.' She then showed me her gravestone and I could read that she had passed over two years before.

"Where is Tina buried?" my client asked. This was the test question. I looked her in the eye and told her that her pet was buried with her Mum who had passed over two years ago, and that the two of them were with us now.

"I wish I'd come to you first," she said. "It would have saved a lot of money!"

I replied that this was her lucky day because I was not going to charge her, I was just so glad to be able to make the connection and help the lady to find some peace. In support of the other mediums, I repeat that we simply cannot bring a spirit through if they are not ready. Perhaps I was just lucky, or perhaps Tina had thought, 'I'd better stop my Mama spending so much money to make sure I'm all right.' And by the way, I was able to tell the lady that Tina's name tag and bell were about three yards away from where she was hit. With that, she went on her way a happy and relieved lady.

Sometimes, though, pets don't come through in a reading; despite my best efforts, the connection is not guaranteed and there are number of reasons for this. If you are feeling very upset or depressed, or just have a lot of things on your mind, it may be difficult to make the link. One of the most common reasons is an emotional block – you have just lost your furry friend and are really suffering with grief.

Some people seem to think it should be easy to connect with an animal's spirit, but the conditions do have to be perfect or it doesn't happen. In fact, what often does happen is that some-thing completely different comes, perhaps another pet or even a relative's or neighbour's pet. Most of the time, things go well. And by the way, a good medium should never ask the client for information or 'lead them on' in any way, but if a medium asks for your pet's name they are only trying to make the connection. It is easier, with animals as with people, to link with a spirit if we know their identity.

I have so many animals coming through to me, both alive (when I'm trying to find them because they're lost or stolen) and deceased. The ones in Heaven tell me there are angels, spirit guides and power animal spirits with them, and say most animals are in 'soul groups' consisting of family members. In my experience, it is usually family members or an angelic being who will come through with them to bring a message. I hear an animal's message telepathically.

Wanting to know about Heaven and how things work, I have done a deep meditation. I did my usual routine of preparation, including psychic protection especially, then set my intention ready to journey into the unknown.

The vision began with a wooded pathway along which were lots of Red Admiral and other butterflies who seemed to bring the message, 'We are with you.' The pathway turned a sky-blue and it felt like I was floating, completely peaceful. There was the scent of roses and candy, a gentle breeze was blowing and I heard... yes, light laughter. I saw what I thought were wood nymphs, like fairies with translucent wings, as I came to a river of crystal clear water.

When spirits, both human and animal, have come through to me and described such places I used to think that surely it cannot be that wonderful, but I take all that back. Here, I saw so many beings with both animal and human in their soul, their love and warmth pulling me in like a magnet. Animals in spirit can take other forms and are not bound by the limitations of one place; it is only when they want to appear to a human, I have learned, that they have to seek permission from a higher being.

As I moved along through this amazing ethereal woodland, a wolf appeared by my side and I asked him, 'Are you my power animal spirit?' He didn't answer and just walked with me in silence, leading me to a craggy outcrop with emerald green grass. I sat down and he sat beside me. Somehow – it's difficult to explain in words – he looked like a human animal. Then I heard a chirping noise and looked round to see a being, more or less in human form, holding out his hands. There were many birds all over his arms and shoulders.

'It's time to go now,' said a voice from somewhere. I was in awe of what I had been shown, so many things I had only heard or read about before but now much more vivid and real. Yet to be truthful I was becoming a little scared: how would I get back home? This was all so utterly different to normal earthly life, so indescribably beautiful, the colours brilliant; but even so, we are always nervous when we're out of our comfort zone. And this was way beyond it.

Then in the blink of an eye I was back in my room wondering whether this was a dream. Yet the sense of deep calm and the connection with my animal spirit guide sitting beside me have stayed with me and will do for the rest of my life. So have no fear for your beloved pet after they have left this world: they are loved and cared for in Heaven, a place of extraordinary peace.

Was that being I saw an angel? From my own years of personal experience and study, I do know that there are many angels and archangels who care for us and our pets[7]. I have a special relationship with Archangel Chamuel and have called upon her many times in these past years for support. When my Mollie was ill, I asked Chamuel to help with her fits and to keep her pain-free. The day before she died, I clearly saw a pink aura around her, a clear sign of Chamuel's presence.

---

[7] See *The Angels Beside Us* for descriptions of the angelic hierarchy.

🐾 Archangel Chamuel · She has a pink ray that especially helps to develop the heart chakra, bringing empathy and banishing negativity. So call upon her support during life-changing events such as grief and loss. Archangel Chamuel prepares everyone to receive the consciousness of the Holy Spirit.

🐾 Archangel Raphael · He is the Master Healer, sending his energies of the green healing ray to our pets who are ailing or in distress.

🐾 Archangel Ariel · The angel of nature, the overseer and fierce protector of animals. Ariel is often depicted alongside the natural elements of the physical world: earth, air, fire and water. Her ray has been described as a rainbow of colours and she often walks alongside Archangel Raphael to heal animals.

🐾 Archangel Fhelyai · She has a beautiful ball of sunshine as her ray and is the angelic communicator, tuning into souls and supplying endless support. Archangel Fhelyai is the first angel our pets see when they pass over, ready to heal and nurture their soul.

A meditation to meet your pet

If you have lost your beloved pet to the spirit world, you may like to try this meditation to reach out to them. First, make sure that you will not be disturbed and that you are sitting or lying down comfortably. Some people like to light a candle, burn incense or play soft spiritual music.

It is important that you are psychically prot(
I call upon the archangels Michael, Raphael, Uri
protect me at times like this and I also ask my s]
Feather for further protection. If you don't know)
be sure that they are nearby so just say, "Dear sp
be here with me and protect me." To focus on the mind, concentrate on your breathing for a while, at least five slow, deep breaths.

Now imagine yourself entering a wood where there is a path to follow. The sun is shining and you feel warm and safe. Then visualise a brightly lit clearing with a large stone in the middle for you to sit on. Rest for a moment and wait.

There is a gate in front of you. It begins to open and you see your pet coming through, nearer and nearer, and you hold out your arms as they come closer. Maybe there's more than one so, as they gather, you greet them and talk to them. What do you want to say? Be patient and allow them to connect with you telepathically. They may even ask you questions themselves so be prepared to answer them. Eventually the animals will fade away and your spirit guide will bring you back to where you started.

Once you are aware of your room again, it is important to thank the angels and your spirit guide for protecting and guiding you. Before going back to your normal day, be sure to 'ground' yourself again with slow breathing, moving your arms and legs and taking a glass of water.

When our pets have passed to the afterlife they can certainly still communicate with us and this can be very emotional. We had a fox terrier called Paddy who would wait for the post each day, then he would fly to the door – we had wooden floors so sound he made was very distinctive – and rip the post to bits. Sadly, he was only seven when he died from a heart complaint.

Only a couple of days after he had died, I heard the post box rattle and then heard the unmistakable clatter of little feet. Letters were sticking out of the box but then they just fell to the floor as though 'someone' had pulled them out. When I got there to pick up the post, the envelopes were ripped around the edges and wet… a bit of an unusual way for our Paddy to let us know he was still around.

Many people say that they have dreamed of their pet. Was this 'just a dream' or could it have been a spiritual experience, the animal sending a message? There is a way to tell the difference because spirit dreams are vivid with beautiful, out-of-this-world colours. The animal may telepathically be giving a clear message they are doing fine and you are not to worry, and they may show you another pet who is deceased and now with them. When you wake up, you will remember a dream like this and remember every word that was said.

One of the other common ways that pets use to tell us that they're still alive and well is to leave their fragrance. We all have our individual scent about us and with pets it is often the passing of wind that we can identify! But you may even hear their collar jingling and it's quite common to see their favourite ball roll across the floor by itself or find another toy moved from where you had left it.

A white feather floating down in front of you from nowhere, just when you're thinking of your pet, is a sign that they're nearby. White feathers always mean that your loved ones in Heaven are watching over you and reassuring you that all is well. Pink feathers are a reminder of the unconditional love the angels give you whilst black ones are a sign that you are perhaps stronger than you think and have reserves of inner wisdom.

For generations, people have believed in special signs and think of them as spiritual messages when they come at particularly significant moments. Robins are thought to be the souls of the departed, come to reassure you that you will have great happiness in your life. Rainbows are seen as representing hope and a bridge between the Earth and Heaven. Seeing a rainbow signifies new beginnings, or a sign that a loved one is happy in the afterlife, so many people are comforted by seeing a rainbow after a funeral. Butterflies represent transformation and the Red Admiral especially, with its vibrant reds and browns, is thought to mean that someone is sending you a message from Heaven. Some cultures believe that butterflies are the souls of children who want their parents to know that they're happy.

The spirits of animals often appear as an image of their former bodies or faces, or some other recognisable feature. Thoughts, emotions or pictures from their lives, or whatever shows their connection with their human companion, may flash into your mind. You may even see a pet's face in the clouds, your mind forming the image to let you know that they are with you.

Animals do want us to know that they're still alive and well after they have left this world. They don't want us to feel despair, even if we sometimes can't help it. We want to think that our furry friend is somehow still with us, and they want us to know that it's true.

7

All in a Day's Work

I was looking forward to my annual leave, two whole weeks, and we were off to Bridlington. My friend Vera called me one day and asked if I'd like to earn a bit of extra money for the holiday; we had trained together and then worked in the same hospital.

"I've done two nights looking after a lady," she said, "but I can't do tonight so will you do it? The only thing is, don't wear your best uniform and shoes because the house is scruffy and she has a few animals." Well, we had worked in the most difficult hospital wards so surely nothing could shock me…

Mrs Dutton lived in a five-bedroom detached house in an affluent part of the city and I felt quite proud as I stood at the front door in my nurse's uniform with my cute little hat, quite the professional. A woman answered the bell.

"Where's the other one?" she asked abruptly. "She walked out last night."

Typical Vera, I thought, she's dropped me in it again. I was shown into the front room where Mrs Dutton was in her bed, looking like a little doll, suffering from cancer. She was surrounded by animals: two cats and two dogs were lying on the bed with her, their muck was on the floor and the room stank.

"We don't want any nurses here anyway," the woman said rudely. "We're looking after her. Still, now you're here you can clean up the dog muck because we aren't doing it."

Another woman hovered in the background. Hmm, these were unusual 'carers', I thought, before pointing out that I had come to nurse Mrs Dutton, not clean up her animals' mess. Still, being me, and because I care about the animals' welfare too, I did clean it up then went into the kitchen to wash my hands. Underneath the sink was a little dog who had given birth to two puppies, although sadly one was dead and there was blood all around. I told Mrs Dutton and asked her what she would like me to do.

"Get rid of the dead pup then clean Cindy and bring her to me," she said weakly. This evening was not exactly turning out as expected; here I was feeling very proud in my nurse's uniform and supposed to be looking after an old lady, when instead I'm cleaning up dog mess, looking after a bitch who's just had pups and 'getting rid of' a dead one. Well, I sorted out Cindy and took her with the live pup to Mrs Dutton, whereupon a male dog started to growl at me, jumped off the bed and into the kitchen, and brought the dead pup back with him. This dog seemed to know more than me just what was going on here.

I washed and changed the lady and gave her the prescribed morphine so she could sleep, but she had an aura around her that clearly told me death was imminent. I was beginning to feel a bit scared about the whole situation so I asked the two women whether they were staying with the lady all night.

"We're here to watch that you don't pinch 'owt, 'cause she has her handbag in bed with her an' it's got thousands of pounds in it." The hairs on the back of my neck stood up now and I definitely did not like how things were developing. I got Mrs Dutton a cup of tea, wrapped the dead pup in newspaper and put it in the sink where the dog could not get it, and as I walked back into the room I saw a blue-silver light above Mrs Dutton's head that swirled around to Cindy. I knew they would both pass over during the night.

Before long, the poor lady's breathing began to change so I asked one of the women if they had her doctor's 'phone number. No, they didn't, raising more suspicions. It was two o'clock in the morning now but I had to call Vera and thankfully she knew where to find the number, in a cupboard along with Mrs Dutton's son's number, so I rang them both. The doctor arrived an hour later and the son five minutes after that. The two women suddenly had personality transplants and one said sweetly, "Shall I make us all a nice cup of tea?" I will not repeat here what I was thinking.

I laid Cindy beside the lady, brushed the other cats and dogs off the bed, and sat with her holding her hand so she wouldn't be alone at the end. First, I saw Cindy's little soul rise up and leave. The little puppy had also become very quiet so I checked on it to find it was also dead. Mrs Dutton's pulse was now weak and her colour and breathing changed; then I saw a white, shining light around her and knew that an angel had come for her. The doctor certified that she had passed over.

With decades of experience in A&E I am used to seeing death so was still thinking clearly, and I suddenly remembered that Mrs Dutton had all that money in her handbag. I told her son and he immediately went into the room just as one of the women was pulling the handbag out of the lady's grasp!

"Just who are you two?" he challenged her.

"We are her carers," she mumbled.

"Carers? Mum never had any carers. I've been away a week on business and I only arranged for the nurse to come. Did Mum employ you?"

The woman confessed that they had just been delivering some brochures when they heard Mrs Dutton call out that she needed help, so they'd stayed 'to look after her'. The son shook his head, dismissed them, and they walked out glaring at me. He asked me to remove his mother's rings for him – they were sapphires, diamonds and emeralds – and I spoke softly to the lady (because I believe the dead can still hear and see what we're doing) saying how sorry I was about all she'd been through but at least she would now be together with her pets. Then I washed her again, the male dog howling all the while.

The son said he would bury the dead animals, take the dog home with him and that the neighbours would have the cats. Then he gave me fifty pounds and thanked me for all I'd done. I put my coat on and just as I was leaving the room I heard a faint 'Thank you' from Mrs Dutton too.

Next day I told Vera what had happened and she came clean: "If I had told you what they were like, you wouldn't have gone." At least I'd got a bit of extra money for my holiday. But a year later I noticed a familiar name in the announcement of Wills in the local paper, saying that Mrs Dutton had left two million pounds. Sometime after all this, she came through to me in a private reading and said, 'Thank you, I have Cindy with me.'

Our minds are very powerful but it wasn't just clairvoyance that helped me in that situation. My intuition had been working overtime, keeping my head clear and letting me know that things were not as they should be. We should all pay attention to our night-time dreams too, because the spirit world may be giving us messages. There was one occasion when I believe an animal's spirit reached out to me.

At the time we didn't have a pet dog because we were all working and it wouldn't be fair to leave it alone at home all day. One night, I clearly dreamed that we had a white and brown terrier who was alone and unwanted, so we kept him. Just a week later I was on my way to work when a pickup truck carrying scrap metal stopped beside me and the very dog I had dreamed about was sitting in the back on top of the load. I knew something strange must be brewing because the dreams I remember have always proved important.

A fortnight later, as he was leaving for work my husband Frank mentioned that he'd seen a little white and brown terrier that seemed to be living at the back of the fish and chip shop, eating scraps that people gave him. Later, I was going to say "Let's go and pick him up" but I didn't need to because at eight o'clock on this cold, snowy evening my daughter Karen walked in with him. He was covered in wounds and it looked like his ears had been cut with scissors. Karen said he'd been hit by a car and was lying in the road, so she'd picked him up and brought him home to be looked after.

We laid the little lad down in front of the coal fire and my heart went out to him, so emaciated and weak. Somehow I knew he was going to stay with us. At the time, I was making beef stew and dumplings for supper and the little dog lifted his head and sniffed the air, so I spooned some of the food into a dish for him. After he'd eaten, I bathed his cuts and whispered to him, "No-one is going to hurt you ever again, little lad."

"We'd better ring your Dad," I said to Karen. Frank was on a late shift and in the manager's office when I called and told him, "Um, we have a dog." The 'phone went quiet for a moment and then he replied through gritted teeth, "Okay, I'll see when I get home."

When he arrived, the dog was still in front of the fire and he lifted his head up to look right into Frank's eyes. "Don't give me that," he said. "You're not staying, laddo." But when he sat down to have his supper, the little chap got up, put his head on Frank's knee and again looked into his eyes. Frank smiled and patted his head.

We called him Benji and he stayed with us for ten years. He became Frank's shadow and they would go for walks in the nearby woods every day; it was soon evident that he'd been used by his previous owner for catching wildlife.

We'd had Benji for a couple of weeks when I called at the fish and chip shop and asked the owner if she remembered a little white and brown dog that fed off scraps at the back. She said he'd been thrown out of a pickup truck filled with scrap metal. The driver had just driven off and left him. I told her, "Well, I have him now so if anyone asks about him you don't know where he is!"

We were all still working so my mother-in-law Flora, who lived across the road, said she would look after him. She spoiled him rotten. When I was ready for work at eight o'clock in the morning, I would say to him, "Go off to Nana's" and he would trot off without looking back and bark at her door until she let him in. When she became ill, he would lie on the bed with her, and when she died he would sit at our gate, very subdued for weeks. Benji himself eventually died of a tumour.

I have a friend who's a brilliant medium and who didn't know anything about Benji or Flora. One day she rang me and said she had a message for me from someone called Flora: "I have my little lad with me and he's better now." His spirit had reached out to me when he was in trouble and it made me happy to know that he was now at peace.

Another dog devoted to his master was a little border terrier who tried hard to save the man's life. Maureen told me that her kids really wanted a dog but her husband was allergic to the hair so she had to say 'No'. One day her hard-working husband came home and flopped into his chair, saying, "What's wrong with me? I feel completely drained." He looked very pale too, but all the doctor's tests came back negative. Every day, things seemed to be getting worse and he began to suffer abdominal pains too.

Because this was upsetting for the children, of course, Maureen said they relented and got a rescue dog for them, a two year-old Border terrier who'd been kept locked up in a shed. The whole family loved her, but the great irony was that she wouldn't let anyone cuddle her except Maureen's husband. She seemed to become obsessed with sniffing his stomach, resting her head there or pawing at the area.

He was growing weaker all the time, losing weight and developing a yellow tinge to his face. The little dog stayed with him and, watching her strange behaviour, Maureen began to think, 'This dog knows something.' She called the doctor again and insisted on further tests; her worst fears were confirmed when they came back indicating that he had stomach cancer that had spread to his liver. It was now clear that the dog had been aware of this, and perhaps was trying to warn them, but it was now too late and sadly the gentleman died a week later. Maureen found a little comfort in knowing that their 'beautiful girl' had given him some joy while he was ill.

Yet the story doesn't end there. Barely a week later the van from the rescue organisation drew up outside the house. At first, the children were worried thinking that they'd come to take the dog back; instead, they watched in amazement as a French bulldog jumped out and was led to their door.

"Your husband called us a little while ago," said the lady, "to say that if we got a French bulldog you would have her so the children could have a pet each." The children believed that their Daddy had sent this dog from Heaven for them. It was sad that his cancer hadn't been discovered in time, despite the terrier's attempts to alert them.

Another clever dog with a talent for diagnosing medical conditions was Samson, a German shepherd with beautiful soulful eyes. I met him when I had just finished a reading at a lady's house and she made me a cup of tea; Samson came in and lay down with his head on my feet. As so often happens, we never know other people's real stories, do we, until they are able to tell us and this one was truly fascinating. I asked whether she'd had him as a puppy.

"No, he came from the RSPCA who had taken him in after his master died," she said. The gentleman had lived alone and the neighbours only realised that something was wrong when Samson had been barking for a couple of days. The police found that the man had died.

"The poor dog must have been starving too," I said.

"Oh no, he had dragged the box of dog biscuits over to his owner and then lain down on his chest. When the RSPCA came, Samson was growling and baring his teeth, but they managed to get him off and take him away." Here was another case of a loyal furry friend caring for his master at the end, yet it turned out that Samson was genuinely psychic too.

"I'd known his master quite well," the lady said. "He had a mobility scooter and Samson would walk alongside him. We got into conversation one day and he told me that the dog kept touching a dark mole on his leg, sniffing and even licking it, so he decided to tell his doctor about it. Samson must have known something was wrong – it turned out to be malignant skin cancer."

At this moment, I felt the atmosphere around us changing and getting cold, and Samson began to wag his tail. I looked around to see the spirit of an old man standing there; he tipped his hat to me and then vanished.

"Samson came to me," the lady continued, "because I'd known him and his master. A good thing too, because he saved my life. I was fit and healthy but Samson would keep jumping up on the sofa and start pawing at my breast. He would sniff it and then start whining." Samson was so insistent, and remembering the story about his master, she had checked her breast and found a lump. She went straight to her doctor and tests showed that it was cancer.

"Samson definitely knew," she said. "And if he hadn't alerted me to it, I would never have known. Yes, he saved my life." She said she now lets Samson sleep on her bed and she feels very close to him, gives him the best food and walks three miles a day with him on the beach.

My own husband has reason to be thankful to a clever dog too. Even though I'm a trained nurse, I sometimes don't notice real problems at first because life is busy and aches and pains are normal.

As I've mentioned, Frank used to very active, walking five miles a day with the dogs. This activity gradually slowed down as his breathing wasn't too good. So one hot day he was in the garden wearing shorts, helping me to plant our vegetables for the next year. As we sat discussing which plants should go where, our fox terrier Jake started pawing at and licking his left leg. Jake was a serious, no-nonsense dog, not at all fussy, but even though Frank pushed him away he started to whimper and sniff his leg again.

This made me take a closer look and I realised straight away that Frank had a deep vein thrombosis, his leg hard and swollen. Then he admitted that the leg had been causing him pain lately. We went to A&E where they not only confirmed he had a DVT but tests also revealed pulmonary embolisms on his lungs. He immediately started medications, which continue to this day. But if it wasn't for Jake, things could have been far more serious.

I never know who or what is going to come through when I give a public demonstration, and I am often surprised. One afternoon I was at a tea room with an audience of about a hundred people – and almost as many spirit animals. The first one in the queue was a beautiful, colourful parrot who told me that her name was Sage.

Her owner, she said, had gone into hospital and someone had left the cage open. "Of course, I flew out into the road but I was killed there." I asked the audience whether anyone had owned a parrot and a man's hand shot up.

"That's me," he said. "I went into hospital and my wife left the cage door open. Stupid woman." I told him that Sage was here now and he replied, "Bugger me, how has she got here?" I thought the best thing to say was that she had flown here to let him know that she was now safe. 'And I'll be waiting for him when he passes over,' added Sage. The man was thoughtful for a moment and apparently wanted to test me.

"We have done something we said we never would," he began. "Does she know what?"

'They have a boy now, named Walter,' Sage told me. The man just shook his head.

"Unbelievable," he said, staring at me. "Who told you that?"

"Sage did," I countered, then moved on. But the tests continued…

Another man was sitting holding a dog collar and looking down at the floor. My attention was moving away from him when suddenly a beautiful Welsh terrier came through to me and said, 'That's my Dad, Lesley.' I asked the man if that was his name, which he confirmed and then demanded to know how I'd found out.

"Your little Lester told me," I said.

"Our Les is here?" he asked, with a look of scepticism. "Okay then… so when I had him put to sleep, what was he wearing?" Lester gave me the information.

"He was wearing a black and white bandana with skulls on it." The man nodded and gasped, as did most of the audience. But Spirit wasn't finished with Lesley yet because now a spirit lady came forward too.

'Tell Les I am here with all our terriers. My name is Joan.' I relayed this message.

"That's my sister," he agreed. "We bred Welsh terriers together." Then Joan showed me a whole pack of terriers, each wearing a bandana with their name on it. Lesley was shocked by this evidence and it seems I had passed the test. I'm just glad he didn't ask me to name all the other terriers.

Clairvoyance isn't the only method for communicating with the spirit world and very occasionally, for whatever reason, it doesn't seem to work as well as usual. Fortunately, thanks to my Grandma Mac's teaching, I have other ways and these were important when a man named Wayne came to see me because his Staffordshire bull terrier had gone missing while out walking. He told me tearfully that Zeus was black and white, not the normal brown and black colouring of this breed, and that he'd chased a rabbit into the woods and disappeared.

"I have a bad back so I couldn't catch him," he said. "And we hadn't walked in that area before so I have no idea where to look for him." He had contacted the local rescue and dog wardens but so far without result. At least the dog was microchipped so hopefully someone might find him and take him to a vet. Wayne was heartbroken because he lived alone with Zeus and he was the man's 'heart and soul'. He pulled out a photo of him and Zeus together looking so happy, and the smile in that dog's eyes for his master was immense.

The atmosphere was tense as we began the reading because I think Wayne expected me simply to zoom in and tell him where Zeus was. I did know he was still alive because there was no spirit connection, so I sent up a silent prayer to 'please help me find Zeus'. At first, the reading was very productive as a man in spirit came forward, saying he was going to help, whom I described to Wayne.

"That's my Dad," he confirmed. "He was my best mate. He had cancer and knew his time was limited so he went out and bought Zeus for me because he knew how devastated I'd be losing him." I could now tell by the smell of burning wood that my spirit guide was beside me.

However, the reading was becoming more difficult, my connection not clear. So I asked Wayne if I could make him a cuppa and then read his tealeaves. He was grateful for this but so was I because it allowed me a breather. This was proving to be a difficult case to solve, unlike the usual messages being passed on by a Mum or Dad.

Thankfully, when I started to read the tealeaves there was loads of information in his cup: the letters Z and W were together, there was a newspaper, a discarded dog collar with studs on it, a cage and some coins as well as the letters B and S and what looked like a compound of caravans. Now, Wayne lived in a completely different part of the country from me and I knew nothing of his area, so at first I just passed on all I'd seen.

Then Dad came back into the reading to say, 'Tell him he will get Zeus back' and he showed me the page of a newspaper with sales advertisements on it. It came to me now that Zeus had been found by a man, not stolen, and he'd been kept in a cage on a travellers' site before being sold. Wayne should put an advertisement in his local newspaper asking for information and he would be contacted by a lady with the initial B.

Some intuition told me to use my pendulum to try and locate Zeus more accurately and this is how it went:

"Has Zeus been stolen?" No.

"Did someone find him and keep him?" Yes.

"Was he at a travellers' site?" Yes.

"Has he been sold to a lady?" Yes.

"Does she have the initial B?" Yes.

Now my normal clairvoyance kicked back in and I was shown a place whose name begins with A… and I checked it with the pendulum. It began to move very fast and soon we knew exactly where Zeus was.

"It's up to you now, Wayne," I said. "Better get your skates on."

He called me three days later and said, "I have Zeus back! I put the advert and his photo in the paper like you said and a lady called Beverley 'phoned me. She had bought him off a man in a pub for a hundred pounds so I gave her a hundred and fifty." He sounded so happy to be reunited with his furry friend. "Zeus is sticking to me like glue," he said.

Yet as so often seems to happen in these cases, there was a real (forgive me again) twist in the tail.

"We are dating now," Wayne went on, "and her initials are BS. How do you do theses amazing things? I never believed in psychic stuff before but I'm forever in your debt. We always keep to same route now when we go for walks but I have Bev by my side so if he runs off again she can catch him."

"I did have a bit of help from your Dad," I replied. "Look, why don't you buy one of those long extendable leads? Then you won't have to let him off."

"It's okay," he said. "Bev is in the local running club so she can catch him!"

A year later I got a call from Wayne to say that he and Bev were having a baby – and Zeus was also a father to four pups. It's strange how fate works out, isn't it? Not so long ago Wayne was feeling completely lost and now he was overjoyed at becoming a Dad and having his best furry friend back by his side.

8

My Bobbie

This is a story I didn't think I would tell and hoped that I would never have to. One day my daughter had looked out of the window and said to me, "Mum, look at that old lady going past, trying to walk her dog. She's struggling to breathe." She was walking with a Zimmer frame too, so we rushed out to see if we could help her. Karen told her that we lived just a few doors from her and if she liked we could take her little dog for a walk with our dogs.

"He hasn't been for a proper walk in two years," she said, "so yes, please."

The following day I called for Bobbie; he did look a bit puzzled when I asked him if he wanted to go for a walk. When we brought him back, Ann had put some chunks of cheese in his bowl because that's what he loved, and I offered to bring him some sausages as I'd cooked some for our terrier Jake. That did the trick. After this, Bobbie would often call for sausages with Jake and I was glad he had some nourishment at least since Ann could not look after him properly due to her respiratory problems. She was really grateful.

We would take him out every day and he loved riding in the car, sitting on my knee. When it was coming up to Christmas we invited Ann and Bobbie round to share our dinner and in the days afterwards we did our best to look after Ann. But she became very ill and was taken to hospital.

"I have been waiting for someone who will look after my Bobbie when I'm gone," she said when we visited. "Now I've found you." She died a couple of days later and her solicitor contacted us to say that Bobbie had been left to me in Ann's Will. He fitted into our family so well. Ann had said he was nine years-old, and now I had him chipped, groomed and vaccinated. His character really came out and he loved his treats and walks.

But we only had him for two years and two months. One Monday morning when I got up, he kept staring at me and then started to croak very loudly, so I picked him up and we took him to the vet. A heart monitor revealed that he was in heart failure and dying. He'd had no symptoms at all, and only three weeks earlier the vet had checked him over thoroughly and passed him fit. They tried every-thing they could, but he passed away peacefully in my arms within hours. To say I was devastated is an understatement and anyone who has lost their pet will know the pain in your heart is unbearable.

After the sad trip to the crematorium we went for a walk with our other dogs, and I asked Ann for a sign that Bobbie was with her. As we walked down the lane, two Red Admiral butterflies flew in front of our faces, then a white angel feather drifted down and around the corner were two robins tweeting away. We were happy to accept these as signs from Ann.

Even now the pain of losing Bobbie is still very raw. My friend Ali Mather, who is a fantastic psychic medium, saw how distressed I was and offered to give me a reading.

"I have Bobbie here," she said, "and he's come through with Ann. She thanks you for looking after him and says his spirit wants to stay with you and Frank and the other dogs. He is in your house and with you when you go for walks." Then Bobbie himself had a message for me.

Bobbie

"I was old and it was my time to go. You held me when I died and there was nothing anyone could do. I am with Frank constantly—" my husband was quite poorly by this time "—and I guide him. When the time comes for him to pass over, I'll be with him."

I had felt Bobbie still around us. Just three days after he had gone, for example, I'd had a bad headache and gone to lie down. Jake was lying with me and suddenly started to wag his tail, then I felt the bed sink as though 'someone' was walking on it and there was a gentle thump into the back of my legs. Bobbie would always come and lie in the curve of my legs. Karen then also had a dream in which she saw Ann holding Bobbie and another black dog; this was later verified by one of Ann's friends who said she'd had a black dog before Bobbie. I was able to find some peace after this, knowing that Bobbie is still with us in spirit, and I tell him every day how loved he was.

As a teenager, I was just beginning to understand how intelligent animals are and how they communicate with one another and with us. My Uncle Alan, the kindest man I ever knew, worked at the local pit looking after the ponies that toiled day after day carrying coal in heavy buckets on their sides. Grandma Mac would pack his lunch with apples and carrots for the ponies and it was my job to deliver them at one o'clock. When the ponies saw me walking down the lane they would whinny because they knew I had their lunch too.

But one day there was no sound and I saw one of the ponies lying on the ground with the others standing silently in a circle around him. I could tell that Billy had broken his leg. Uncle Alan was in the office so I ran as fast as I could to find him. When we got back, I held Billy's head gently while we waited for the vet; his soulful eyes looked into mine and I knew he was passing away. The other ponies then all started neighing, low at first and then louder, quite scary.

One of the ponies was missing. Billy always worked alongside another pony called Dante, who was nowhere to be seen. But just as Billy was taking his last breaths, Dante reappeared round the corner and came over to us. He nuzzled Billy and then let out a very loud roar of grief at losing his best buddy. The pit ponies were retired soon after this accident.

I realised then that animals do see the pain of other animals and know when they are sick and dying. The ponies knew their buddy was going to the spirit world, and Billy knew that his friends were around him at the end, keeping him safe.

Not every bereaved owner wants to replace their pet but sometimes life has a way of giving us what we need – and even more besides. Andrew contacted me after his Blue Staffordshire bull terrier died from kidney failure, hoping I could connect with Archie. I had to explain that the dog's spirit may not come through because he had only passed over recently, but Andrew seemed to take this as some kind of excuse.

"Yes, my friend said this was all a load of tosh."

"Give me a chance," I replied as patiently as I could. "I'm not going to be interrogated here. I work with Spirit to bring loved ones through and hopefully pass on a message." At this he seemed quite embarrassed and apologised.

"Sorry, I don't know about this sort of thing."

"And neither does your friend by the sound of it," I smiled.

"I lived on my own with Archie, never had a girlfriend and he was my soulmate."

Andrew was clearly emotional and I thought to myself, 'I have to do good for this lad.' So I called on Black Feather and my power animal spirit, and straight away I was shown images of Archie, a rather fat bull terrier with only one eye. I passed on what I saw to Andrew and he was obviously shocked, taking a sharp breath in.

"Oh my God, that's my Archie," he exclaimed. "You really are genuine." He went on to tell me that he had rescued Archie from a man who organised dog fights and that's how he'd lost his eye. Andrew was adamant that he didn't want another dog. Moreover, he had seen three other psychics before me, all of whom had failed to contact his pet, so he was very upset.

I told him that Spirit was showing me the letter J and the number 21, and that he would be getting another dog in unusual circumstances. The letters D and T were significant. "Oh, and Archie is telling me that he's a Dad."

"No, that's impossible, he can't be. He was with me all the time, and I only left him once to go to hospital with my sister— oh heck, she has a bitch that isn't spayed…"

The reading continued and I was given the name Corky, another dog who was with Archie. Andrew confirmed that he'd had another dog who had also passed away suddenly; he'd been called Corky because he let out horrible farts and Andrew would say "Cork it" to him! Then a male spirit appeared, wearing a flat cap and with a cigarette hanging from his lips. (No, I don't think cigarettes are on sale in the afterlife – this was for identification.)

"That's my Dad," said Andrew. "He even went to bed in that flat cap. He only died four weeks ago. We were inseparable and I was always telling him off for smoking. I said those things would kill him. Well, they did, he died with lung cancer." Then Andrew paused and looked around, saying that the room had gone very cold and he could smell cigarette smoke. He was definitely less sceptical now.

His Dad asked me to pass on the message 'I love you, son' and showed me an odd image of a mannequin wearing a flat cap. Andrew said that he had his Dad's cap on a mannequin head in the sitting room. As the reading came to a close, I repeated the message that another dog would be coming into his life in three weeks.

"Sorry, you're wrong about that," he insisted. "I could never love another dog as much as Archie. Still, you've been spot on with other things."

Five weeks passed and guess what? Andrew called me to say that his sister's dog had had four pups, and one was born with 'cherry eyes'. (This is a prolapsed gland in the eyelid.) This was in the left eye, the same eye that Archie had lost. The pup was named Arthur.

This was a good result but not the end of the story. A few years later, I was walking my own dogs when a Blue Staffy with one eye ran up to us with Andrew running after him. He said he had lost my 'phone number and was so glad to see me. He told me that Arthur had had to have his left eye removed because of an infection, and his behaviour was exactly like Archie's, even pulling his master's socks off and sleeping with his head under the pillow.

"And by the way," he went on with a big smile, "DT is my fiancée's initials and we're having a baby in a couple of months. You brought me much happiness that day."

"You're no longer a sceptic then, Andrew?"

Andrew's story, like many others, shows that with the help of Spirit I am often able to bring hidden information to light as well as reunite people with their pets. But some cases seem more like detective work, especially when the client is not telling me the truth! A tearful lady called me to ask if I could find her two Ragdoll cats, Star and Luna, who had gone missing from her conservatory four weeks earlier. She said they were house cats and never normally went outside so she was sure they had become lost.

"I was only gone two hours, taking my Mum to hospital because my sister was working and couldn't do it," she said, dabbing her eyes. "It was a very hot day so I opened the conservatory windows, and when I got home the cats were gone." She added that Star and Luna were very valuable and that Luna was having kittens. My first suspicion was raised when she said that despite this she hadn't reported the matter to the police.

The tough thing about a reading concerning animals is that their spirit might come forward when the owner doesn't know they have passed over, so then the stress falls on my shoulders to tell them. I decided to use my Witch Tarot cards because I usually get more information with them but in any case I was able to tell the lady that I couldn't feel the cats in spirit so they were alive. She didn't seem too surprised by this, or even relieved.

Next, I silently called upon Black Feather for help and straight away he told me that the cats were in danger. I didn't relay this to the lady yet because she was very edgy and I didn't want her disturbing my visions. That didn't last long, though.

The first card was the Page of Swords, which I never like to see, and I had to tell her that the cats had been stolen and that this had all been planned. There was a young man involved and a money motive. Someone had known the lady's movements and had been waiting for an opportunity.

"Oh, they didn't jump out of the window, then? But who would steal them?"

A spirit man came forward now holding a Ragdoll cat and saying the word 'Dolly'. This was my client's father, who had bred Ragdolls when he was alive.

"Dad," she shouted, "please help me find Star and Luna!"

'They are not her cats,' he replied.

"Okay, I bloody well know that, Dad," she snapped in a nasty tone. I told her that if she acted like this we would lose the connection because the spirit world is very sensitive and, sure enough, the candle I had lit as I always do for this work blew out. We had lost the connection with her Dad.

"Sorry, Dad knows how stressed I get. We never got on."

The Moon is the card of deceit, signifying that things are not always as they appear and confirming my earlier suspicion. I was shown a vision of a red van and the same young man I had seen before, with a blonde woman who was holding both cats and smiling at him. The word I heard was 'groomer'. Still, when I asked the lady if she had seen such a red van, perhaps with the word 'Groomer' on the side, she shook her head.

The next card was the Six of Swords which suggests some sort of trouble with water. When I told the lady this she seemed to have become very withdrawn and silent, which is strange because people usually want to know every nugget of information about their pet. By now I was sure she was holding back and knew who had the cats.

"Are you sure you have no idea who should steal your cats?" I asked. Her Dad then came back and said, 'It's her sister.' So I pressed the lady, "Is your sister a hairdresser? I've just been given that information by your Dad. She has your cats and has had their hair cut off."

"All right," she admitted, blushing. "What you say is true."

Then the most awful thing happened. I felt fur brush my legs and when I looked down there were four little eyes looking up at me. Dad told me, 'They've been drowned.'

I felt sick. How was I now going to tell this lady that her cats were dead? This is always the worst part of my work yet I must be honest. I said I had some terrible news from her Dad, that Star and Luna had been drowned and I was so sorry. She didn't believe me so I had to ask her to contact her sister, since her Dad had spoken to me and I had seen the two cats in spirit.

"I haven't spoken to my sister for two years since Dad passed over," she said quietly. "She went on holiday and I looked after the cats but then I refused to give them back. It was all-out war.

We argued and Dad tried to come between us but he had a heart attack and died. It was all my fault."

Her father then came forward again and said, 'They're with me now so neither of them can have them.' At this, the lady started to cry and said, "I am so sorry, Dad. Please look after my babies and their babies."

Now that we knew who killed the cats, I asked my client if she was going to inform the police, but she said that her nephew was training to be a lawyer and could lose his career if she did. She said she would go to see her sister and 'give her what for'.

That was a really tough and emotional reading, especially with such secrets coming out, and it really upset me. And how wicked it was to drown two beautiful furries just out of jealousy. I did hear from the lady a year later, though, and she sent me a photograph of two cats identical to Star and Luna. Her sister had apologised for her jealousy and admitted asking her son to drown the cats because she was angry and grieving for their Dad. So she had bought her sister the two new cats, who were called Moonie and Skye. In the end, I suppose, it was their Dad's intervention that reconciled the family and saved the day.

Another case of stolen pets was also both very trying for me and involved hidden information. A young lad and his Mam came to see me wanting to know if I could shed any light on who had stolen two caged gerbils from their house. The boy had been asked by his teacher to look after them during the school holidays. I thought it unlikely that I would be able to help, but I would try to locate them and the thief. The boy was really upset and couldn't stop sobbing, whilst his Mam was shouting at him and calling him stupid.

She told me that they lived in a rough area and always had to keep their doors locked because of the thieving that went on in the neighbourhood. The boy had gone out to play on his bike when one of his mates had called for him and it seems he forgot to lock the door. He started to wail again and his mother clipped him round the head.

"I can't trust you with your own key," she said. "Give it to me now."

"I lost it," he sobbed.

"It has your — name on the fob," she raged. "Anyone can get into the house now."

I was getting upset myself with all this so I tried to reassure the lad that I would try my hardest to find the gerbils. Then I suggested I make us all a cuppa to calm down and went into the kitchen for some deep breaths and to ask Black Feather for help.

After five minutes I was shown a vision of a woman hiding the gerbils' cage under a blanket, then there was a dark coloured car and the number seven. The boy's mother said she had no idea who the woman was when I described her. I knew that the number seven had to be significant because Spirit don't show me random things. Then I was shown the inside of a pet shop and a For Sale notice above the gerbils' cage. There was only one pet shop in town so my client thanked me and said she would drive straight there.

She told me later that, yes, the gerbils were indeed in the shop and the owner had said that a woman with a young lad had brought them in. She'd said that her son was allergic to them so he gave her forty pounds for them. My client explained the situation to him, that they belonged to the school and her son was looking after them until they were stolen, but he wasn't going to give them back. So she'd had no alternative but to give him the money.

A week later, the kids went back to school and she was waiting to pick her son up when she was taken aback to see the woman I had described standing in front of her with her own son, who was wearing a number seven football shirt. She'd decided not to confront the woman because she'd heard that her husband had left her with three children and she was selling off her jewellery to buy food.

"I had a crafty plan," she told me. "I invited three of his friends and the lad with the football shirt to help me find my son's key, saying I thought it must be on the local playing field.

I said that whoever found it would get ten pounds. Well, it was cheaper than having locks changed. We'd been walking around the field for less than ten minutes when, sure enough, the lad in the number seven shirt said he'd found the key!"

She had the culprit so the next thing was to tackle his mother, who looked horrified when she opened the front door. My client said the police had been called (which was a bluff) and asked her why she'd stolen the gerbils. The woman started to cry and confessed everything.

"I knew you worked," she'd said, "so I waited until you went out and sent my son to call for your boy, then I went in and took them. I was desperate. My husband took off and left us with no food or money, and I have three kids to look after. I'm so sorry."

My client said she'd been invited in but there wasn't even any furniture to sit on. She'd given the woman twenty pounds to buy food for the kids, since I hadn't charged her for finding the gerbils. It was a sad situation that ended well, because the women became best friends.

Earlier, I described how Gypsy Rose Lee would read tealeaves and this skill was taught to me too by my Grandma Mac. Back in the early days of my nursing career, the word somehow got out and I would be pestered by my colleagues to the extent that there was soon a regular slot for readings during my dinner break. One woman sat down across the table looking very worried, and proceeded to really test my patience.

"You are my last hope to find my six stolen chickens," she said. "They've been stolen from right under my nose. They are champions, too, and I was showing them at an agriculture show." Well, I had always assumed that people kept chickens for their eggs but not this lady – one of hers was worth over a thousand pounds. She went on to tell me that she was a 'fancier' and, seeing my blank face, explained with a touch of irritation that this is what poultry breeders are called.

"Shall we look into your cup, then?" I suggested. "It may take a while to see the visions, though." At this, she pulled out a fortune telling book and asked if I'd like to borrow it! "I don't read from books," I pointed out. "Spirit gives me the visions and the information I need." I seemed to have ruffled her feathers by this but I was feeling under pressure myself by now; I had to find these chickens, otherwise my name would be mud in the hospital.

Fortunately, the shapes in her cup were making sense right from the start. I was shown a classroom with people at their desks and the word 'Pass' was spelled out. This seemed a bit confusing but I told her anyway and she replied that she had just taken the nursing entrance exam. "Well, you've passed, that's good news," I said.

"The only good news I want to hear is where my chickens are," she replied tartly. "So why tell me that?"

As patiently as possible, I examined the cup again and was shown a red hut with a lock on the door, which I passed on.

"It's a coup, not a hut," she said.

Next, a spirit voice said the word 'Buttercup' and I saw chickens' legs with numbers attached to them by the feet.

"Oh, at last we're getting somewhere now," she sighed.

At this point I could feel Black Feather coming forward so I sent out a silent 'Thank you' and 'Help!' He showed me a list of flowers' names and it turned out that all these chickens were called by these names: bluebell, snowdrop, primrose, rose, iris and daisy. The word 'buttercup' was repeated insistently.

"Clever girl," my client conceded. "That's the breed, they're Brocklesby Buttercups."

The story began to unfold rapidly now, like watching a film. The chickens were in cages in a large tent, and while the woman went to an office someone backed up a horse box and put the cages into the back, then drove away fast.

"Right, I know them two," she sat back angrily. "They live on a farm near me and it's the first time they've been to a show. They don't have their own chickens." But as she spoke, I was seeing something else, an image of white cliffs and a boat. "So my girls are going on a boat trip, are they?" she whispered. "Well, I don't — think so."

At this, she was off with no thanks. Sometime later, she saw me in the hospital and called out that she'd got four of her chickens back but two had died. I had been right about the women involved, though, so she now thanked me.

Years after this, I was giving a lecture on wound care to around fifty doctors and nurses and, when it ended, I invited questions. A woman's voice asked, "Are you still reading tealeaves and can I book in with you?" As everyone turned round with surprise, she announced, "She is really good. You should all make a booking."

Dogs, cats, ponies, gerbils and chickens… We are realising that it is not just the common pets who have souls and live on in the spirit world after they leave us. The medium Gina Lorraine Murray tells the touching story of another, rather unexpected feathered friend[8].

"I was in the middle of a reading," she says. "The young woman in front of me sat quite composed as I relayed information from a dearly loved brother who had passed over a year before from a tragic accident. He made it clear that he was well and still very much part of the family's life by giving information of their daily activities to prove he had been with them."

His sister confirmed all the evidence he gave but suddenly, out of the corner of her eye, Gina became aware of another presence right beside her, nestled close to her leg. It was a brown goose! This bird made it very clear to Gina that he wanted her client to know he was there. When she told the previously very calm young woman, "All composure shot out of the window and she was in tears."

This extraordinary bird proceeded to pass on information in the same way a spirit person does, with images, feelings and words. Much of it was extremely evidential. He spoke of his life indoors with the woman, sitting on the settee next to her, and of how he would paddle in the bath and go out with her in the car. He also spoke of a dog with whom he was friends, and his owner

---

[8]   *www.ginalmurray.com*

verified everything, saying that she now felt so much happier than when she'd walked in, knowing that both her brother and feathered friend were alive and well.

"Animals of all species go to the same place as us," says Gina. "There is no question of that. They stay linked to those they have loved and are still loved, and are there to meet us when we pass over."

9

Do Animals Come Back to Us?

We met Kim and her husband Steve in an earlier chapter. She also told me the quite extraordinary story of her second rescue dog, a Cavalier King Charles spaniel. They had seen an advertisement for him, then known as Ted, at a rescue centre. This was when their pet Noah was still alive and they took him with them to meet him. The two dogs got on famously together but the woman who ran the centre was "horrible, a very uncaring, brusque personality." When Ted got too near to her in the fenced-off pound area, she kicked him with the side of her foot. The 'phone rang in her ramshackle office building calling her away, and Kim said to her husband, "Pay her – we're leaving with that dog."

They called him Hamish. The little lad was petrified of strangers and so frightened that he was forever weeing, but gradually he settled down well with Noah and the family. Sadly, he developed pancreatitis and his heart failed. A little while later, Kim was standing by the washing machine when a voice in her head said, 'Find Jasmine' – that was all, and they didn't have a clue what it meant. However, looking online locally, Steve found a Cavalier spaniel named Jasmine at a different rescue centre. They got there as fast as they could and walked into the office to see the dog sitting beside the manageress at her desk. But the lady said, "Sorry, she has just been reserved."

"I ran out sobbing," said Kim, "thinking I had failed the request of Spirit. But the woman followed us and asked us to come with her. It turned out that Jasmine had two puppies who had been born at the centre and they both trotted out towards us. Both were poorly and needing operations, and one of them was already reserved. They visited the other one, Percy, for several weeks until he was well enough for his operation but he would never answer to his name. "It was as though he was just an empty shell with no soul," Kim said.

"When he had his operation, he was struggling to come through it. Steve and I were waiting nervously at home, sitting on the bed, when we both clearly heard a bark. We'd know that bark anywhere, it was our Hamish! It seemed to come from the foot of the stairs but when I went to look there was nothing of course. Suddenly I was stopped in my tracks as a vision came into my mind, showing the soul of Hamish entering the body of Percy. I had to sit down, I was trembling so much, and then I heard a voice in my head, 'You will call him Isaac.' Later, Steve looked up the meaning of the name: 'He who will live again'."

The manageress of the centre rang them to say that Percy had pulled through and they could see him in a week's time. Off they went to meet him properly, feeling both anxious and excited; a door opened and he trotted out happily towards them. He seemed to respond immediately to his new name and licked Kim's face when she picked him up. They had Isaac for nine years, and although he had a twisted spine he was not in pain and despite his early struggles he had the best life possible.

Yes, animals can give us great comfort as well as happy companionship. And it seems that sometimes they can continue to do that even after they have passed away. A little Jack Russell, Minnie, clearly decided to try and ease her owner's grief from the spirit world.

Beverley was distraught when she contacted me and still in shock because she had thought she was only taking Minnie to the vet with constipation. It wasn't clear to her what had really happened to her little friend because the Covid-19 precautions meant that Beverley was not allowed into the veterinary practice with Minnie and had to hand her over to the nurse. The vet later told Beverley that the cause of death was internal bleeding, which they had been unable to stop.

Beverley was inconsolable, having lost her best friend when Minnie was only four years-old. Would I be able to contact her and see whether she was okay?

I was able to bring Minnie through, a beautiful furry spirit with a lovely warm energy around her. She came with an older gentleman who had a large nose and brought a smell of kippers. Beverly confirmed that this was her grandad. A black dog and a budgie had also come along for the trip!

Minnie showed me the scene in the vet's surgery and how hard they had tried to save her but (I heard the words in my head) she had stomach cancer. Then I saw that she had been wrapped in a pink and red blanket when she was taken to be cremated. I told Beverley all this and she said, "Yes, that's true. But it doesn't matter now, my heart is broken." Well, Minnie had some thoughts on how to help with that and telepathically told me that Beverley should watch out for a ball rolling across the floor because that would be the sign she was safe and well. There was more: 'I am sending a new puppy to her,' she said, 'which will have my soul.'

I thought this very bizarre. A while later, I contacted Beverley to see how she was getting on and she told me that a few weeks after these sad events her husband had bought her a new puppy. Minnie had a black heart shape on her body and this new puppy, Leila, had exactly the same marking and in the same place. Moreover, Beverley said that her characteristics were just the same as Minnie's.

Minnie had died on the 26th October and Leila was born on the 28th October. Could it really be true that when pets pass over their souls can sometimes pass into new-born animals, who then have the same characters and personalities?

When I was writing these extraordinary accounts about Hamish and Minnie, whose souls seemed to return in the bodies of new puppies, it reminded me of when I was fifteen. I would spend happy hours in the wood across from where we lived with my sisters, making daisy chains and picking the petals off, reciting, "He loves me, he loves me not…" My friend Dora would often sit with us with her cat Madge, a big tortoiseshell with oddly coloured eyes, one blue and one green. This cat was forever sneezing so Dora would take out her handkerchief and wipe its nose, while we couldn't stop laughing. Dora adored Madge and would sometimes even put her in a doll's pram, dressed up like a baby.

One hot day, Dora had put a matinée coat on Madge along with a bonnet, which I thought was too much in this weather, but Dora said that the cat kept shivering. Then Madge started to shake violently and Dora was screaming, so I ran to fetch her Mum. When we got back, the cat had died in Dora's arms. She was hysterical and my sisters were also frightened and crying.

A passing man said, "It's only a bloody cat, pull yourself together." From that day, whenever I hear someone say words like that I get angry: these animals are someone's beloved furry friends. Dora's Dad buried Madge in the garden and Dora was so upset she hardly left the house for three weeks, often saying that she could see Madge in the garden. I didn't know what to make of this so I told my Grandma Mac, who said, "Let's pray for her little soul and ask God if he has any spare cats to send to Dora."

Six months later, Dora asked if we could go for a walk together; I had to visit my auntie first so she came with me and we sat for a while drinking some pop. Auntie's neighbour came around to see her.

"That's another kitten gone, thank God," she said. "I think we might have to drown the last one. Nobody wants it because it's got odd eyes, one blue and one green. And it keeps sneezing— what?" Dora and I were staring at her and we asked if we could see the kitten. It was the absolute image of Madge and Dora asked if she could have it.

"Every night I prayed to God to send me a kitten," she said to me on the way home. "He answered my prayers." I had done the same thing every night. She happily took Lily the kitten in the pram for walks every day and, yes, it did keep sneezing just like Madge. The vet found that it had a sinus problem, which was soon rectified. Like Hamish and Minnie, had Madge been reincarnated?

There are widely different viewpoints on the subject of reincarnation and I can only describe my personal experiences with clients, as I have done here. Naturally, I have come across many people who have lost their beloved pet and some will buy another animal to compensate for their loss. Perhaps some are so heartbroken that they try to 'recreate' their lost pet, kidding themselves that their new pet is a reincarnation of it.

For myself, I have come to believe, based on years of experience reading for clients, that reincarnation can happen. So then I started to wonder how long it is likely to take for a pet to be reborn. After extensive research and guidance from Spirit, I learned that it all depends on what the animal's soul chooses to do, but in general it can be months or even years. It is entirely up to the animal to decide whether they want to come back or stay in the safety of the spirit world – and it doesn't matter how much they might have been missed by loving owners. It is the individual soul's decision and not one to be taken lightly, especially if the animal had been very sick, neglected or abused. After all, consider this: if you found yourself in the spirit world, in beautiful surroundings, cared for and free of all illness, would you want to come back here? But if an animal makes the request to do so, then Spirit will make available different lifetimes to choose from.

Have you got a new puppy, for example? And do you recognise things about the pup's appearance or behaviour that remind you of your previous pet? My daughter Karen and her husband Rehaz tell a story about just this.

They had rescued two West Highland terriers, Molly and Tessie, both six years-old. Molly was a fiery little dog who loved Rehaz unconditionally and was very possessive of him. She went everywhere with him, sleeping on his shoulder, always licking his left ear – not the right ear, it had to be the left one. They'd had the dogs for four years when Molly started struggling to walk and eventually they made the heart-wrenching decision to have her put to sleep.

Two years later, they decided to have another dog though not necessarily a Westie. They applied for a few dogs on rescue websites but for one reason or another none of them were available or suitable. One day, Karen was looking for something else on her iPad when a farm selling Westie puppies flashed up, two hundred miles away in Wales. Still, they decided to go and see the puppies. Four pups were for sale, and immediately one of them simply made a beeline for Rehaz, refusing to leave him alone, jumping on his knee and licking his left ear. "That was a sign," says Karen.

She was very thin and undernourished, but they bought her and called her Millie; their other Westie, Tessie, got on with her straight away and Millie had found her forever home. Then as she began to grow, she would mimic things that Molly had done, like lying on Rehaz's left shoulder and licking his left ear. She hated bath time, just like Molly.

Yet there were more extraordinary 'coincidences'. The dogs had their own food bowls and Tessie had always had a blue one, but since Molly's death she had insisted on using Molly's red bowl. When Milly arrived and was given the blue bowl, she overturned it onto the floor and went to eat out of the red one. The dogs also had lots of special toys and Molly had particularly loved her duck; guess what, the first toy Millie picked out was the duck and it remained her favourite toy. It isn't hard to believe that Millie is a reincarnation of Mollie.

When a much-loved pet passes away, a lot of people feel a big hole in their lives and look for another furry friend. As we have seen, the new arrival can sometimes have striking similarities with the animal that has gone before and there are definitely many strange accounts of this.

I seem to have the kind of face that invites people to talk to me, especially when they are elderly and alone – and have a story to tell. I had just finished my shift in A&E one day and was feeling really tired, sitting in the bus shelter with an old lady and wishing the bus would hurry up.

"Can I tell you about my budgie, Boris?" she asked. "It's just that I don't see many people to talk to." I hoped I wouldn't nod off while she told me about Boris and she must have seen how exhausted I was, offering me a glucose sweet to perk me up.

"My son bought Boris for me," she continued, "because my husband had just died and he thought it would be company for me. He was very handsome with a yellow tuft on his head, but he was a noisy little devil, always chirping. The only thing that kept him quiet was a glucose sweet, same as I just gave you. He would sit on his perch and shake his feathers, spread out his wings and just give one chirp to tell me he wanted a sweet." I had never heard of a bird eating sweets before and said that Boris sounded quite a lively character.

"Oh yes, he was. He would turn his red water bowl upside down and sit on it, knowing he would get my attention." I had now picked up on the word 'was' and realised that Boris had died, then as I began to listen more intently I saw a spirit bird perched on her shoulder. "But something terrible happened," she went on. "I used to let him fly around the room but one day I forgot the kitchen door was open and he flew out. I called out to him to come back but he ignored me. Then he landed on next door's fence and their cat jumped up and killed him." I said how sorry I was to hear that, but the lady hadn't finished her story and was becoming quite animated.

"It was three months later, my son's budgie had babies and they were blue, like Boris. He said I could have one so I went round to his house. There they were, three babies all blue except one had a yellow tuft on his head just like my Boris. It started chirping very loud so I picked him up and it chirped again. I took him home and called him Sirob, that's Boris spelled backwards."

I stifled a yawn and said, "That's a lovely story—"

"Oh, I haven't finished yet. I put him in Boris's cage and do you know what he did – he tipped the red water bowl over and sat on it chirping loudly. So I gave him a glucose sweet and that shut him up." She paused for a while, smiling to herself, then said, "Thank you, nurse, for listening. You're very kind to bear with an old woman wittering on about her born-again budgie."

I was actually quite glad that the bus was running late.

Some spiritual people are even able to link with their pet in a psychic way and become aware of their past lives together. Sandra Bray is an author[9] and Reiki animal healer who describes her special relationship with her German shepherd.

"I met my companion when she was a three month-old puppy. She came straight to me and sat with her head on my feet, then looked right up into my eyes. Our next encounter was just over a year later, when she did the same thing and her owner said, 'She's not really a guard dog…' Two days later she joined my life. There has always been a strong bond between us right from the start. She has a strange habit of sitting on my feet and a particular dislike of crows. I called her Twosocks, after the wolf in the film *Dancing with Wolves*; it had been the last outing I'd had with my brother before he died.

"I attended a workshop with a trance medium whose guide told me that I had lived a previous life with her, when I was a Canadian Inuit and she was a husky dog. During meditation I sent a request to Twosocks to show me something of our past life together. I had a vision of a wooded area where a European man

---

[9] *Odd Days of Heaven* and *Even More Days of Heaven* (Local Legend, 2016, 2018)

114

wearing leathers and furs was aiming a long musket at me. I was in a snowy clearing with my husky sitting on my feet. I was killed instantly with a shot to the head and she stayed with me to keep the crows from scavenging my body.

"In another meditation later, I asked her why she had come to me at this time, and received the answer, 'Because you are on your own.' We have become inseparable, she swims in the sea with me and trots alongside when I'm cycling."

It's strange how we seem to be guided to our pets sometimes, as though it was all meant to be. All my own dogs have been rescues except one, my boy Rebel. We were visiting a relative whom we did not see very often and he happened to mention that his dog, Bessie, had had pups again.

"I think the father is an Irish wolfhound," he said. "It was hanging around a few months ago. There's only one pup left. It's a bit funny-looking with a lump on the top of its head so no-one wants it." Well, we'd only gone there for a courtesy visit but I knew straight away that I was taking that puppy home, though I hadn't even seen it. I thought, 'What the heck if it does have a lump on its head, this dog belongs in our family.'

When the shed door was opened, the most beautiful sight met me. The little chap was suckling his Mam but he turned round to look at me with enormous brown twinkling eyes, as though to say, 'I am ready to go home now.'

The medium and author Jenny Smedley has also written[10] about the past lives of her dog KC, a black springer spaniel Labrador cross. She says that KC was formerly Ace, her German shepherd Labrador cross. Before that she was a dog owned by a Comanche boy called Peyote, and her soul had also been in the body of a wild black bear Jenny encountered in the USA.

These accounts raise interesting questions about 'soul groups' – where several spirits, both human and animal, may share several lifetimes together in different roles – and 'transmigration'. Belief

---

[10] *Pets Have Souls Too* (Hay House UK, 2009)

115

in animal reincarnation dates back at least as far as the ancient Egyptians and Greeks (taught by Pythagoras for example) and some Buddhists, Hindus, Taoists and Judaic cabalists embrace the theory. Some within these religions go further and speak of soul transmigration (also known as metempsychosis), the belief that the souls of the deceased may pass into different bodily forms. In more modern times, the concept is also associated with the philosopher Nietzsche and is a theme of James Joyce's *Ulysses*.

My research has taught me that there are seven stages in the process of reincarnation. Once a soul ends their life cycle there is the initial 'transition' to the spirit world, then periods of 'renewal' or healing and of 'learning' from one's experiences and from spirit guides. Now there comes the offer of 'decision' and consideration of what form to take, the 'manifestation', followed by 'reflection' on everything that has been learned and agreed before the final 'restoration'.

There are no set time periods, as we experience time, for these stages to be passed through. The soul itself decides, if you like, when the time is right. It seems reasonable to think that if a pet died of old age it may take longer to come back into the physical world, if it chooses to. However, if the pet died young, they could reincarnate sooner and into a similar role as before. Fate may decree, in some instances, that your new pet is a reincarnation of a previous one... but we just don't know the full truth of these things. And we certainly cannot control them, we cannot 'wish' a beloved deceased pet back to us.

It is only fair to say that there have been many eminent thinkers who disagree entirely with these beliefs, including spiritualists! The international spiritual medium Andy Byng[11] says that, "... mediumship provides insufficient evidence of animal survival. Alongside the intellectual difficulties that such a claim creates, spiritualists ought to conclude that animals do not survive physical death... [T]he more astute may argue that principle seven[12]

---

[11] *https://www.andybyng.com/*
[12] This refers to the *Seven Principles of Spiritualism*, the last of which is 'Eternal progress open to every human soul'.

suggests animals are immortal, but are unable to progress once they are in the spirit world... Most eminent thinkers did not believe in animal immortality.

"It is generally accepted," he continues, "that animals do not communicate with mediums directly. Instead, information relating to a pet is given by a spirit person, which suggests that the spirit communicator uses the dog as a piece of evidence, rather than the dog surviving physical death."

Well, the accounts given in this book would beg to differ with that. But Andy does nevertheless also say, "I do hope my claims are wrong..."

One sceptical eminent thinker was Sir Arthur Findlay, one of the great pioneers of modern Spiritualism, who stood firm against reincarnation. And the long-time highly respected Editor of *Psychic News*, Maurice Barbanell, was also a non-believer who would write in his columns that every case of reincarnation could be explained as a 'spirit possession' rather than a rebirth. This was despite those who attended his trance mediumship séances reporting that his spirit guide, Silver Birch, regularly proclaimed the truth of reincarnation!

We might also turn to Saint Augustine of Hippo who said that, "...to be alive is to have a soul, and death involves a process leading to the absence of the soul. Therefore, not only do human beings have souls, but so do plants and other animals."

Having read the stories in this book, I hope you will agree that animals do indeed have souls and may reincarnate. Undoubtedly, the debate will rage on. I leave the last word here to Roy Steadman, an equally respected successor to Maurice Barbanell as Editor, who is reported as saying, "In my judgement, reincarnation is the explanation that best fits the facts."

10

Animals That Heal Us

The earlier stories of Jake, Samson and others, show that many animals can sense illness in us and even draw our attention to the particular part of the body that needs investigation. Have you ever wondered why your pet snuggles up to you when you are ill? I can vouch for that. I have bouts of very bad pain when I cannot walk or sleep and have to lie on my bed, taking lots of pain killers. My two dogs refuse to leave me at these times, and even others' offer of a walk do not move them.

When I was a teenager we had neighbours who were disabled with arthritis so I helped them out whenever I could, taking their two Jack Russells called Jack and Flash for a walk in the woods near where we lived. One day the lady said, "Mester is in bed poorly, so I'm very grateful you taking them out." 'Mester' adored those dogs, the children he'd never had.

But both dogs were acting strangely, whining at the bedroom door, and when I tried to put their leads on they started howling and sniffing the air. I knew something wasn't right because they loved their walks but didn't want to leave the house today. We finally got outside but they kept looking back at the house. They would usually be off chasing rabbits but now they just slunk along quietly until, after about a mile, they both suddenly stopped and let out a loud howl together.

We eventually came out of the woods and saw the ambulance outside my neighbours' house. Mester had had a seizure while in bed and then died. And from that day, the Jack Russells refused to leave the house even for a walk. These two dogs had known that their Mester was going to die and they didn't want to leave him. Did they detect the scent of some changes in his body or was it a sixth sense?

Science informs us that our pets are more than a just cuddly friends. Cats and dogs in particular release a subtle energy into the atmosphere that encourages the release of endorphins in our brains, easing our aches and pains. Russian researchers have monitored molecular changes in the atmosphere, producing a kind of neurological homing device that lets an animal know when we are poorly. We have four-legged healers with us, without ever realising it.

Doctors and care home owners are waking up to the fact that having a pet or two is certainly life-enhancing. A study carried out at the School of Veterinary Science for the Animal Society of Canada concluded that Alzheimer's disease patients are less aggressive and anxious, and more coherent, when they are introduced to a friendly cat or dog. The effect can become noticeable within thirty minutes of meeting the animal. I had experience of seeing this when I worked in the Chest Unit. A consultant would bring her own little dog with her on her rounds and Alzheimer's patients were much easier to treat then, their mood improving dramatically.

The chartered psychologist Dr June McNicholas with a support team from Warwick University also found that we don't visit our GP as frequently as we used to when we get a pet. Moreover, long-term depression can be alleviated simply by having dogs around.

Kimbo is a very special dog who comforts bereaved people. An undertaker's wife told me that he is known as their 'comfort companion'. She had heard of dogs in America called 'funeral therapy dogs' that were popular, so did some research and introduced Kimbo to their funeral business. He knows instantly if the people coming in are there to visit their deceased relatives, and without prompting will actually accompany them into the viewing room. Then, as the funeral arrangements are discussed, Kimbo will sense the relatives' grief and sit in front of them while they stroke his head. He will often put his head on one person's lap and then move on to the next person. Many families have told the undertaker that Kimbo has really helped them deal with their grief. Several studies have confirmed that the presence of a dog can lower our blood pressure and promote the feel-good hormones such as serotonin, dopamine and oxytocin.

I have mentioned that my daughter Karen has always loved horses and definitely has a way with them, somehow being able to 'tune in' and communicate with them. When she was sixteen and studying to become an equine teacher for disabled children, the stables where she kept her horse had a partnership with Riding for the Disabled. One day, the owner of the stables asked Karen if she would take three disabled children out riding, warning her that "They are very noisy and somewhat unruly."

Karen let them choose their ponies, which were called Biscuit, Jigsaw and Dapple, and explained to the children that they must wear riding hats, whereupon one of the girls grabbed Dapple's mane and bit him on the nose. But then the children each put their arms around their ponies and were soon trotting off happily. They rode through the local woods with their carers and when they arrived back one of the carers said, "It's like a bloody miracle – the kids were so happy they never made a sound." That wasn't the end of it either because the children then fed their ponies with carrots and apples and gave them a brush down, their faces glowing with joy. The manager of the Children's Home reported that these youngsters remained calmer than before and would talk every day about their ponies.

Karen had prepared well before the lesson, communicating with the ponies and asking them to behave and be gentle with the children on their backs, giving them each an apple to seal the deal. Riding for the Disabled helps people both mentally and physically. The horse's rhythm moves a rider's body in a manner similar to the human gait and this encourages mental stimulation, flexibility, balance and muscle strength, apart from the emotional benefit.

There is a fifteen year-old French horse called Peyo who does medical rounds with doctors. His owner competed in equine events and noticed that Peyo seemed to seek out anyone in the arena who was disabled or unwell. Soon the horse and his owner were allowed to visit patients receiving palliative care and they would stay with them as they passed over. Before he enters a ward or hospice, for hygienic reasons Peyo's hair is braided, his hooves greased and his body covered in lotion and a blanket. Then he trots around the corridor and lifts his leg when he wants to see a particular patient. This wonderfully intuitive horse can sense when a human has cancer and homes in on those most in need.

The impact he has had on these patients has been astounding, soothing those undergoing treatment for metastatic cancer to the extent that medical teams have nicknamed him Doctor Peyo. These end of life patients require less medication, allowing for a peaceful passing. One day, Peyo saw a man whom he knew from previous equestrian events, now in hospital suffering from cancer. The man is reported as saying, "When I see my beautiful friend Peyo, my heart sings and I feel much better." When this gentleman passed away, horse and owner were invited to the funeral; Peyo stood over the coffin and gave a few low grunts, probably saying his goodbyes to his loving friend. Peyo has supported around a thousand people in the last few years and veterinary experts have examined him to try and discover just what makes him so special. No-one yet knows.

Some animals show their love in less obvious ways yet the emotional and healing effect can be dramatic. Alexis was suffering from a serious illness, in extreme pain with Crohn's disease and having chemotherapy treatment. Despite being in very difficult circumstances, she came across a skinny, starving stray dog who looked at her with fearful brown eyes.

"I knew I was going to save this dog's life," says Alexis, "but little did I know she was about to save mine." She called the dog Maggie.

Alexis had been stacking heavy boxes one day when she collapsed with exhaustion and felt like she was dying, but Maggie came to lie at her side, never moving until she could get back up again. Still, Alexis says that she felt "at the peak of misery" because her marriage had broken up and she was really sick. Sitting on the floor, she reached for a knife intending to kill herself but Maggie jumped up and licked her face. This simple act made Alexis feel guilty and determined to be strong for her furry friend.

Alexis knew that being around animals made her happy so over time she took in several more abandoned and sick dogs. When Maggie finally developed a lung tumour and passed over, Alexis set up an animal hospice in her name, determined to give love to others in her memory so that they could die with dignity[13]. It opened in 2016 and received twenty thousand donations in just the first year. The hospice has been a peaceful home for cockerels, turkeys, sheep, dogs, cats, hens, pigs, a quail and a disabled lamb called Gimli who discovered a love for Rich Tea biscuits.

A similar story is told by Laura about her dog, Patch, saying, "He is the reason I get up in a morning." Laura sadly lost her Dad and her own young daughter, and has PTSD. She says that Patch wasn't breathing when he was born and she saved his life, but her furry friend has more than repaid the favour, becoming both her support and an 'alert dog'. He knows when she is feeling particularly anxious and will come up to Laura and kiss her, putting his paws around her. When she lost her father and daughter, he came to the funerals too. Even more than this, Patch literally saves Laura on a daily basis: she suffers from epilepsy caused by a brain tumour and Patch knows when a fit is imminent, lying down close to her as a warning and helping her to cope.

---

[13]   *https://www.themaggiefleminganimalhospice.org.uk*

"He goes everywhere with me now," says Laura. "He is the reason I am still here today."

Seven year-old Molly was a street dog in Thailand who'd had hot oil thrown over her. Somehow she survived and was rescued by the Soi Dog Foundation who nursed her back to health with years of love and care. Her new owner, Yvonne, says that now Molly has in turn rescued her from the deep depression of losing her Mum. Molly has now been honoured as a 'Super Dog' for her extraordinarily loving behaviour.

A golden retriever, Sindy, also saved a life in heart-stopping circumstances. Brenda was at home with her two daughters, Nicola aged six and Sarah aged three, who were watching TV cartoons while their mother did household chores. Sindy was snuggled up with the girls. Brenda went outside at the back of the house for a few minutes and when she got back Nicola came running up to her and said, "Sarah's gone." The front gate was open too, despite always being kept bolted, and Brenda began to panic. Then her world stood still as she saw her youngest daughter just about to step off the pavement into the path of fast-moving traffic.

Suddenly there was a rush of wind beside her as Sindy raced past, ran in front of Sarah and pushed her back onto the curb. "It was a miracle," says Brenda. "Someone in Heaven was looking out for us that day. Our beautiful golden Sindy saved my Sarah's life."

It seems amazing that so many people dismiss animals as 'lower creatures' not worthy of our care and respect, presumably on the grounds that they cannot talk as we do and haven't evolved in the same ways as us. As we saw in the last chapter, even some of the greatest thinkers and spiritual leaders deny that animals have souls. (This book is my attempt to change that thinking!)

Quite apart from the countless stories told by honest, everyday people about communication with the spirits of their deceased furry friends, what simply cannot be denied is that many animals have important skills that humans lack and a 'different', yet highly developed, kind of intelligence to ours.

Over the years, it's become clear to me that this is true. (Perhaps we used to have these senses too, but lost them when we became 'civilised'!) Our dog Mollie was a Daddy's girl, she followed my husband Frank everywhere and she'd sit on his walking boots at two o'clock, knowing they would soon be off walking in the dense woods near to where we lived.

One day, it was getting dark and I started to get a bit worried, then Frank rang to say that Mollie had got lost in the woods. She was only two years-old then and surely wouldn't know how to get home, so my neighbour took me out and we searched for ages with no sign of her. Now, my daughter Karen lived on a busy main road with fast traffic at all hours of the day, and she also had a dog, Clyde, whom Mollie adored. As we drove down Karen's road, there was Mollie sitting patiently on the front step.

What was unbelievable, though, was that Mollie had never been to Karen's house before! Did her good friend Clyde sense the danger and 'send her directions' to keep her safe?

When I was a nurse working on a Chest Unit, several of our patients were miners who knew one another from their community. Nearly all of them kept homing pigeons and took great pride in telling us stories about their champions and the races they'd won. Twice a week, I would escort one gentleman with cancer, Ted, to another hospital for radiotherapy and he would tell me about his birds as we travelled.

"I was brought up in a mining village," he said, "so we all followed in our Dads' footsteps down the pit when we were old enough. My Dad taught me about pigeons too, how to look after 'em and race 'em. I did thirty years. It was hard, lass, after a shift in the belly of the mine all I wanted was to get a pint of beer and see my birds." Seeing my face, he laughed and said, "No, not the wife and kids, the pigeons!"

At that moment, I felt the presence of a spirit man in the ambulance and we both heard a cooing noise. "Bloody 'ell, they're calling me," Ted said. The spirit looked at me and said, 'Dad.' He was wearing a flat cap and was the image of his son.

"I have over thirty birds in a loft on the allotment," Ted went on, "but my champions are in a hut in the yard. I bring 'em in every night in case someone steals 'em, my Jocky and Flash."

After his treatment, Ted looked terrible and was sick all the way back to the Unit so I put him to bed and asked him if we wanted anything. He whispered, "Yes, to see my birds before I die." The Sister agreed that his wife could bring the birds in as long as they were kept in the cage, which she did the next day. We had to tell her that Ted was very poorly and his treatment wasn't working so he was just on strong pain relief. But he was elated to see his beautiful prize birds and wanted to show them off to all the staff.

The spirit man reappeared again so I knew Ted didn't have long left. I left them all together for a while, then Ted's wife walked into the office and said, "You're the nurse that sees things, aren't you?" Her friend had heard another nurse talking about me so I had to hold my hand up. "The reason I ask is that I saw Ted's Dad yesterday. He was in my room at home so I'm wondering if he's come to fetch him." I told her what I'd seen and she confirmed that it was her husband's father.

Early the next day, Ted's breathing deteriorated and he was dying. In his room, I saw his spirit Dad again and then heard a loud cooing sound. His two prize birds were sitting on the windowsill outside! I telephoned his wife to let her know what was happening and she said she'd let the birds out inside the house but someone had opened the door and they'd gone. I told her not to worry, I was going to try and catch them, which I did with a bit of coaxing. Relieved, I put them in Ted's arms. His wife arrived just as he slipped away.

Well, these pigeons are trained to come back home after a race. But Jocky and Flash clearly loved their master as much as he loved them and, after only one visit, managed to find their way to his hospital window to be with him in his last hour. These two went on to win many more races, no doubt spurred on by Ted and his Dad.

We often think of pigeons as a nuisance and rats as dirty and rather scary little things. Well, Magawa has been described as a 'Hero Rat' and awarded a Gold Medal for his gallantry and devotion by the UK's People's Dispensary for Sick Animals (PDSA)! This furry chap has detected over seventy landmines and about thirty unexploded munitions, clearing an area of more than 41,000 square metres in Cambodia and thereby saving hundreds of lives.

It is estimated that some five million landmines were laid in that country during the war years 1975-1998, causing over sixty thousand casualties. When the war ended, the massive task of making the land safe again began. Magawa, among others, was trained by a Belgian NGO not only to detect mines but also to 'sniff out' tuberculosis.

Rats significantly speed up the detection work because of their amazing sense of smell and excellent memory. And unlike human tools such as metal detectors, they are able to ignore metal and home in on explosives, a more efficient way to do the job – and nearly one hundred times faster than conventional methods. Magawa was trained, from four weeks-old for a period of nine months, to scratch the ground near to a buried device, receiving a tasty food reward for his success.

After five years' work, his performance unbeaten, he is now retired from active duty although will continue to help with the training of his successors. A dumb animal? Magawa is described by his handlers as "a bundle of energy, a real character with a steely determination." Rats are indeed highly intelligent and caring animals, obvious when we observe how they look after their pups and kittens, feeding and grooming them.

Guide dogs for those who have impaired sight or hearing, and police dogs that can sniff out drugs, are such a familiar sight to us that we almost take their intelligence and skills for granted. And as we have seen above, some dogs are able to sense when their owners are ill, even before there are any symptoms. These skills have become critically important to us all now, with the arrival of the Covid-19 pandemic. Could specialist medical sniffer dogs detect coronavirus in humans?

The UK charity Medical Detection Dogs has already trained dogs to detect malaria, Parkinson's disease and various cancers. More than ten years of research by the charity has proved that dogs can be trained to recognise the distinctive odour of a disease at the equivalent dilution of a teaspoon of sugar in two Olympic-sized swimming pools of water. In partnership with the London School of Hygiene and Tropical Medicine and Durham University, they have begun to use Labradors and cocker spaniels to detect coronavirus in humans before symptoms appear.

The training involves collecting odour samples from infected people (from their breath, body odour or facemasks) and from those who are uninfected. The dogs are rewarded for identifying the Covid-19 samples and thus hone their skills over a period of several weeks. If successful, they will be used at airports, testing centres and possibly hospitals.

We owe a great deal to our furry friends and we are only recently waking up to the remarkable intelligence of a wide range of animals. New research has demonstrated that goats can also recognise human faces, especially smiling ones, and rival dogs in forming an emotional bond with their owners, according to researchers from London's Queen Mary University. Indeed, these animals are very attuned to human body language even if they are not domesticated, and "…are smarter than their reputation suggests" according to Queen Mary's Dr Alan McElligott.

For example, it's been shown that goats can work out how to break into a sealed box using levers, a task normally used to gauge intelligence in apes. In another experiment, the box was made impossible to open and the goat's reactions were recorded. They turned towards their handlers "in a pleading manner, clearly asking for help in getting to the treat."

Showing that even animals such as goats, which most of us give little thought to, are highly intelligent and sentient, has great implications for animal welfare. Let's hope that this new awareness is soon extended towards all creatures, great and small.

It is incredibly sad that, for generations, human beings have cared so little for our beautiful planet, exploiting both the Earth and her wildlife for our own short-term benefits. Instead of recognising that we are custodians of other creatures that are not pet material, we have ignored or abused them or hunted many of them almost to extinction. Yet as the accounts here demonstrate, several animals, furry or not, have intelligence and emotional awareness that deserve to be recognised – and even their own distinct ways of communicating with us.

One famous story, although by no means the only one of its kind, was told by the well-known Italian deep sea diver, Enzo Maiorca, a few years ago. He was in the water near Syracuse, beside his boat and talking to his daughter Rossana on board.

Feeling a light nudge in his back, he turned round to see a male dolphin at the surface, very close to him. Enzo was used to interacting with dolphins (sometimes they seemed to want to 'play') but this one was deliberately getting his attention. It swam a short distance away, returned, and swam away again, as though wanting the man to go with him.

He followed the dolphin, diving down to a depth of about twelve metres, where he found a female dolphin trapped in a discarded fishing net. Maiorca quickly swam back to the boat and asked his daughter to come with him, bringing their diving knives. After a few minutes, they managed to free the cow, working fast because a dolphin can only survive under water for about ten minutes.

The two dolphins then came up to the surface and Enzo suddenly realised that the cow was not only pregnant, she was about to give birth. After she had breathed out foam and blood, the calf was born and led to his mother's nipples by the father, guiding it with his nose. Soon after this, Enzo reported, the bull circled him and his daughter then rose up in the water and touched his cheek with his nose "like a kiss of gratitude" before the new family swam away.

"Until Man learns to respect nature and talk to the animal kingdom," Enzo said, "he will never know his true role on Earth." The character Enzo Molinari in the 1988 Luc Besson film *The Big Blue* was based on Maiorca.

Indeed, dolphins have been recognised as very special creatures throughout history and across the world. In ancient Egypt, they were believed to represent the power of the goddess Isis, whilst the Greeks thought of them as almost divine beings who guided the spirits of the dead to the Isles of the Blessed. Amazon river dolphins, known as Botos, are still revered by some tribes as 'shapeshifters' that can take human form.

There are many stories of dolphins saving people from drowning. One of the earliest is that of Arion of Methymna, a famous singer at the court of Periander, Tyrant of Corinth, around 600

BC. Arion sailed to Italy to seek his fortune and then sailed home with his wealth on a Corinthian ship. But the crew plotted to rob and then kill him. He begged to be allowed to sing one last song...

It was a common belief that it was a good omen when dolphins followed in a ship's wake and that they were attracted by harmonious singing. So Arion took up his position at the stern with his lyre and sang for his life. Sure enough, he charmed some nearby dolphins so much that, when Arion jumped overboard to escape the crew, one of them let him climb on its back and carried him to Taenarum in southern Greece, from where he made his way safely back home.

Well, we cannot know how true that one is, but a story similar to Enzo Maiorca's emerged recently of a humpback whale trapped with its tail and flippers entangled in abandoned fishing nets. It was spotted by three men in a boat off the coast of California who initially thought it was already dead because it was floating on the water. But then it blew out a loud breath. The men decided to try and cut the animal free, snorkelling alongside it.

"As I swam alongside the animal, our eyes met," said Michael Fishbach. "There were no words we could share but I wanted to let the whale know we were there to help. The sight of this large and beautiful creature, trapped and so close to death, was emotionally overwhelming." Michael admitted that he was scared because the whale was frightened and fatigued and it could still kill him or sink the boat with one panicked movement.

He got back onto the boat and the three men tried to cut the net off with the small knives they had, it taking about an hour of hard work. They pulled the remaining netting onto the boat so it wouldn't cause more harm. Then they were treated to a dramatic show of freedom and gratitude: instead of simply swimming away to safety, the whale circled the boat for about an hour, breaching about forty times and diving under the surface while waving its tail above the water.

"It was an incredible experience that none of us will ever forget," said Michael.

There is so much that we don't know about life in our great oceans but these creatures are certainly highly intelligent and emotional. They may not be able to speak our language, but they are capable of showing us their gratitude when we help them. They have spirit.

11

Guiding Spirits

"**O**ur world and way of life have to change drastically," says Christa Mackinnon, psychologist and author[14]. She believes that not only have we created unprecedented ecological destruction, but many people feel their lives lack meaning and experience isolation and poor health because we have separated ourselves too far from nature and from Spirit. "We have starved our souls." The remedy is to reconnect with our 'Earth souls', become closer to nature and expand our awareness of its spirit.

An approach that can help is shamanism. One of the oldest forms of spiritual path, shamanism was traditionally a way of working with the hidden energetic forces of this and other worlds. The shaman would enter altered states to connect with Spirit in order to bring health and harmony to their communities – they were the healers, visionaries and psychics for their people.

Nowadays, modern medicine men and women combine traditional teachings (especially from the Americas or Mongolia) with up to date healing methods and a focus on ecology. They

---

[14] *www.chistamackinnon.com*. Her book is *Shamanism Made Easy* (Hay House UK, 2018)

see themselves as "…working towards the expansion of our consciousness for personal healing and spiritual growth and to restore our connection to nature," says Christa.

We need to become whole again. And so does the Earth.

The modern shaman is a bridge between different worlds, connecting body, mind and soul by working with the energies of nature spirits, spirit guides, ancestors and animal helpers. The aim, Christa says, is to "…see ourselves as an integral part of the Earth soul and reconnect with the sacredness of life."

Yet every one of us is able to reach out to the spirit worlds to bring healing, guidance and greater meaning into our lives. We don't need to be shamans or psychic mediums, for we are already aware of the spirits of animals by our experience at home with our beloved furry friends.

A 'power animal spirit' is not the soul of an individual pet that has passed away, but rather the essential spirit of a particular kind of animal: it has the individual characteristics and natural talents of that animal, such as strength, grace or wisdom. For a shaman, the power animal is a guide and protector through alternative worlds, always by their side. Yet we can all relate to particular animals, perhaps because we admire them or wish we could be like them in some ways, and we can invite their spirit to come closer to us in our everyday lives. We can even give them a name, to make the bond stronger.

Sometimes they just turn up in our lives anyway! Something in our unconscious minds draws them to us and we start to realise that we are receiving 'messages'. Maybe a raven begins to visit your garden regularly, or you can't help seeing images of lions everywhere… This could be the spirit's invitation to us to take notice and try to discover what its meaning is. So we need to be mindful of these signs and, with practice and patience, accept the spiritual lesson being offered.

For example, when I was a young nurse, a grey owl began to appear at the bottom of my garden. I didn't take much notice of it at first although I put water and worms out for it. Later, I was walking with my dogs in a different part of the county when I noticed a grey owl sitting on a fence nearby; was this the same one from home that had followed me? It's quite uncommon to see these birds, yet still I didn't think much about it until I was back at work, writing up an assignment for my degree course. I didn't have a computer then and had to do everything by hand.

One of the doctors happened to be passing and took an interest, so I told him that I really needed a nice front cover. A couple of days later I was working with the same doctor and he said, "Oh, I have something for you. My son did this on his new computer." In the envelope he gave me was a beautiful colour picture of a grey owl.

I asked the doctor why he'd suggested this image to his son and he replied, "Because you're wise." I don't know about that, but I realised that the grey owl was a power animal spirit for me.

The owl is a creature of the night with special vision and hearing, so nothing and no-one is hidden from them. Quite appropriate for a spiritual medium. They also offer us the lesson of personal dignity. So if you think someone is being deceitful with you and you are feeling undermined, or you're being forced into a situation where you don't feel confident, call on the spirit of the owl for guidance. (Incidentally, one of history's great healers, Florence Nightingale, had a small pet owl that she'd rescued in Greece. Called Athena, she carried it with her in her pocket.)

Some years later, I had been meditating regularly, asking Archangel Fhelyai for support, when I kept seeing glimpses of a black bear. Then in ordinary life I also started seeing images of this animal, such as logos, frequently and realised he was important. Any doubts were well and truly dispelled when I was asked to give readings at a psychic fair organised by *Identities*, a support group for abused women.

I did fifteen readings that day so had no time to wander round and see what else was going on, but a child's large, fluffy black bear on one of the stalls caught my eye. There was a raffle to win it, with fifty possible names on a piece of paper for people to choose from. By the time I got there, all the names had been taken except one, Madison, so I signed up for that. At the end of the day, all the names went into a hat and a lady pulled out the winner – Madison. One woman nearby grumbled, "Ah, she's the psychic so she must have known." But I had just taken the last name available. The black bear chose me!

I have learned that the characteristics of this power animal spirit are assertiveness and confidence with a preference for doing things your own way. Yes, that's me! The black bear is also associated with healing ability and knowing the secrets of medicinal plants; well, I spent three decades as a nurse and my Grandma Mac, the local Wise Woman, had taught me as a child about using wild plants for healing. Perhaps the bear's most important gift is teaching the importance of strong protective grounding when doing spiritual work. Nowadays, I know when bear is with me by his distinctive woodland scent. But anyone can call upon the black bear's spirit when in need of emotional or physical healing, or wanting his strength to sort out a difficult problem.

Let's suppose that you don't know who your power animal is and you want to look for them in your unconscious mind. One way is through dreaming or deep meditation, because in this state we are free to go anywhere we want. Set your intention in advance and follow this journey:

You are wearing a protective cloak and travelling into a special place in nature, exploring your surroundings. This place seems somehow familiar, the colours are vivid and you begin to sense nature spirits around you. When you feel comfortable, ask your power animal spirit to come forward and meet you. You need to be patient and perhaps repeat this meditation several times, but eventually an animal will come to meet you.

At this point, remind yourself that all animals have their own special gifts and the purpose of your journey is to find what you really need, rather than what you think you want. Whichever animal spirit approaches, you must be willing to welcome them unconditionally and be respectful.

Perhaps more than one animal appears... In this case, ask whether they come with love for you, and don't be afraid because you have that protective cloak around you. Some will go away and only one will remain – this is your power animal spirit.

You may like to ask questions now and the animal will respond by putting images into your mind. They may even lead you on a journey further into their natural habitat where you meet other animal spirits, before returning you to your starting point. Give the animal your thanks and finally take off your cloak.

Having accepted your power animal spirit you have agreed to work with them and try to learn whatever lessons they offer. They will always be there for you so try to be mindful and not block any signs or visions they give you. Many people like to have a 'power object' that bridges the gap between them and their animal, making the connection stronger. This could be a particular stone, a crystal or a small model that you keep in your pocket or on a personal altar at home.

Each power animal spirit has its own qualities and you may like to research them further to learn what they are trying to show you[15]. But you will find that life becomes more exciting when you find your animal guide and know that they will always support you. Always remember that they offer what we actually need, not what we think we need – they come through the deepest parts of our minds – so it may not be the cutest or most popular animal that comes to us.

For example, the humble blackbird is inviting you to follow your spiritual path and expand your vision. You may well be

---

[15] A good reference book is *Power Animals* by Steven Farmer (Hay House, 2015)

a gentle soul but you must also learn to defend your territory, your personal space, and be particular about who shares it with you. The dolphin is a beautiful, loving creature who helps you to create balance in your life; she encourages you to live in the moment and rely more on your intuition. You can call on the dolphin to help you find what is lacking in your life. The frog leaps effortlessly from one environment to another, giving you the strength and courage to be adaptable and accept new situations or relationships.

Some people find themselves meeting mystical power animals rather than the familiar ones of this world. These creatures are fictional, yet they are powerful archetypes that can guide us in important ways. Dragons have a fiery temperament and a powerful determination to protect themselves and, according to tradition, their gold. They give us energy and renewed confidence when we are feeling low, and remind us that the spirit is our greatest treasure and must not be neglected. The unicorn represents purity and honesty, so supports us in living a good life in line with our highest values and morals. Even that strangest of creatures, the griffin – part eagle, part lion and part snake – can be a faithful guide, giving us the strength to make changes in our lives whilst encouraging us to be discreet and more observant of others.

I hope you have enjoyed reading this book and have come to understand, if you did not already know, that our beloved pets have intelligent minds, caring hearts and spirits that live on after they have left us. The stories in this book are evidence of this and of how vital it is that we do all we can to live in harmony with the animal world. Indeed, all animals are deserving of our love and respect and, in many ways, they give us more than we give them.

Like many readers, I have also experienced the devastating sadness of losing a furry friend, going through all the stages of grief. But I know that they are still with us and we can reach out and connect with them, watching for their signs.

Do not stand by my grave and weep.
I am not there, I do not sleep...
Do not stand by my grave, and cry.
I am not there, I did not die.

—CLARE HARNER, 1934

Last Word

Many years ago, I worked on a unit for disabled young adults suffering from life-threatening diseases and accidents. Elle was seriously ill with head injuries sustained when a hit and run driver knocked her down. Her speech was slurred and she could only communicate by drawing pictures, even though her Mum told us that Elle couldn't draw at all before her accident.

One day I was going to take her for therapy and was about to lift her out of her chair when I felt something like an electric shock. The girl looked at me and pointed to my side, squealing with pleasure and grabbing my hand. I turned to see a spirit lady standing beside me, holding a black and white cat in her arms. Elle looked at me and clearly said, "Cat." Now I had a real dilemma: should I admit that I could see the lady and her cat or keep quiet?

She started to breathe faster and become pale so I got her into bed and sat with her for a while. Then she said "Cat" again and pointed to a pile of her drawings; they were amazingly good and, yes, there it was, the same black and white cat I had seen.

This was a dramatic moment because she had not spoken for two years, so I rang the call bell and Sister came running. She wouldn't believe me and said, "It must one of your visions." So Elle said it again. Then she smiled and said, "Nanan." It was one of the most wonderful moment of my nursing career. Not only was my patient getting her speech back, it seemed that she was clairvoyant too!

Over the next several days, the spirit lady was visiting often and I hoped this wasn't because something bad was going to happen. In fact, Elle was doing really well, stringing words together. She would call out "Sally" and then "Cat" again.

Next visiting day, we were out on the veranda playing cards when we saw her parents' car arrive and they got out carrying a black and white cat in a basket. Sure enough, it was Elle's cat, named Sally. Sally was the image of her mother, who had died some time ago. Elle stood up and took a few steps towards them, even though she'd been paralysed since her accident.

Sister agreed that she could keep Sally in her room as long as she went into her carry basket at night. Elle nodded but Sister said, "That's not good enough, I want you to say 'Yes'." So she did.

A couple of months later a young man arrived to see Elle and her eyes shone with love. This was her boyfriend, although until now she'd refused to see him since the accident to allow him to 'move on' with his life. Now we had company on our walks every day around the grounds, with Sally on a lead and the spirit lady often nearby. Four months after this, Elle was well enough to go home and when I cleared out her room I found a beautiful drawing of her Nan, with a black and white cat in her arms, under the mattress.

It was Christmastime two years on when we had a big surprise. At the Carol Service in the afternoon, the doors opened and there was Elle, holding Sally, and her husband, holding their baby boy.

Our pets are not just our furry friends. In this world and from the afterlife, they help us to heal.

If you have enjoyed this book...

Local Legend is committed to publishing the very best spiritual writing, both fiction and non-fiction. You might also enjoy:

GHOSTS OF THE NHS

Glynis Amy Allen (ISBN 978-1-910027-34-9)

It is rare to find an account of interaction with the spirit world that is so wonderfully down-to-earth! The author simply gives us one extraordinary true story after another, as entertaining as they are evidential. Glynis, an hereditary medium, worked for thirty years as a senior hospital nurse in the National Health Service, mostly in A&E wards. Almost on a daily basis, she would see patients' souls leave their bodies escorted by spirit relatives or find herself working alongside spirit doctors – not to mention the Grey Lady, a frequent ethereal visitor! A unique contribution to our understanding of life, this book was an immediate bestseller. Winner of the Silver Medal in the national *Wishing Shelf Awards*. *"What a fascinating read. The author has a way of putting across a story that is compelling and honest... highly recommended!"*

THE ANGELS BESIDE US

Glynis Amy Allen (ISBN 978-1-910027-39-4)

A sequel to *Ghosts of the NHS*, Glynis gives us more eye-opening accounts of her spiritual experiences in her inimitably humble and honest style. Here we read of her many encounters with beautiful and compassionate angelic beings who come to guide us when in danger or to give comfort to the sick. Her life has been dedicated to working in the NHS and with Spirit, and she shares her vast knowledge of the ethereal worlds with us, teaching us how we may reach out to and work with our own guardian angels. This book is warmly endorsed by the renowned 'angel author' Chrissie Astell.

Winner of the Local Legend national
Spiritual Writing Competition.

THE QUIRKY MEDIUM

Alison Wynne-Ryder (ISBN 978-1-907203-47-3)

Alison is the co-host of the TV show *Rescue Mediums*, in which she puts herself in real danger to free homes of lost and often malicious spirits. Yet she is a most reluctant medium, afraid of ghosts! This is her amazing and often very funny autobiography, taking us backstage of the television production as well as describing how she came to discover the psychic gifts that have brought her an international following.

Winner of the Silver Medal in the national
Wishing Shelf Book Awards.
"Almost impossible to put down."

SPIRIT SHOWS THE WAY

Pam Brittan (ISBN 978-1-910027-28-8)

A clairvoyant medium for over thirty years and highly respected throughout the UK, Pam describes herself as "an ordinary woman with an extraordinary gift." Despite many personal difficulties, she has shared this gift tirelessly and brought comfort and understanding of Spirit to a great many people. Here, she inspires us to realise our own innate gifts and to trust that Spirit will always guide us on the right path.

DAY TRIPS TO HEAVEN
T J Hobbs (ISBN 978-1-907203-99-2)

The author's debut novel is a brilliant description of life in the spiritual worlds and of the guidance available to all of us on Earth as we struggle to be the best we can. Ethan is learning to be a spirit guide but having a hard time of it, with too many questions and too much self-doubt. But he has potential, so is given a special dispensation to bring a few deserving souls for a preview of the afterlife, to help them with crucial decisions they have to make in their lives. The book is full of gentle humour, compassion and spiritual knowledge, and it asks important questions of us all.

AURA CHILD
A I Kaymen (ISBN 978-1-907203-71-8)

One of the most astonishing books ever written, telling the true story of a genuine Indigo child. Genevieve grew up in a normal London family but from an early age realised that she had very special spiritual and psychic gifts. She saw the energy fields around living things, read people's thoughts and even found herself slipping through time and able to converse with the spirits of those who had lived in her neighbourhood. This is an uplifting and inspiring book for what it tells us about the nature of our minds.

CELESTIAL AMBULANCE
Ann Matkins (ISBN 978-1-907203-45-9)

A brave and delightful comedy novel. Having died of cancer, Ben wakes up in the afterlife looking forward to a good rest, only to find that everyone is expected to get a job! He becomes the driver of an ambulance (with a mind of her own), rescuing the spirits of others who have died suddenly and delivering them safely home. This book is as thought-provoking as it is entertaining.
"A fun novel packed full of wisdom."
The Wishing Shelf Book Awards.

TAP ONCE FOR YES

Jacquie Parton (ISBN 978-1-907203-62-6)

This extraordinary book offers powerful evidence of human survival after death. When Jacquie's son Andrew suddenly committed suicide, she was devastated. But she was determined to find out whether his spirit lived on, and began to receive incredible yet undeniable messages from him on her mobile 'phone... Several others also then described deliberate attempts at spirit contact. This is a story of astonishing love and courage, as Jacquie fought her own grief and others' doubts in order to prove to the world that her son still lives.

"A compelling read." *The Wishing Shelf Book Awards*.

HAUNTED BY PAST LIVES

Sarah Truman (ISBN 978-1-910027-13-4)

When Sarah's partner told her that she had murdered him, she took little notice. After all, dreams don't mean anything, do they? But Tom's recurring and vividly detailed dreams demanded to be investigated and so the pair embarked upon thorough and professional historical research, uncovering previously unknown facts that seemed to lead to only one simple conclusion: past lives are true! Yet even that was not the end of their story, for they had unwittingly lifted the lid on some dramatic supernatural phenomena...

Local Legend titles are available as paperbacks and eBooks. For further details and extracts of these and many other beautiful books for the Mind, Body and Spirit please visit

www.local-legend.co.uk

Lightning Source UK Ltd.
Milton Keynes UK
UKHW020838300123
416167UK00009B/29

9 781910 027486